ANIMAL WATCH

A Visual Introduction to

BIG CATS

ANIMAL WATCH

A Visual Introduction to

BIG CATS

A Cherrytree Book

Created by Firecrest Books Ltd
Copyright © 2002 Evans Brothers Ltd

First paperback edition published 2002

First UK edition published 2000
by Cherrytree Press
327 High Street
Slough, Berkshire SL1 1TX

A subsidiary of Evans Brothers Limited

British Library Cataloguing in Publication Data

Stonehouse, Bernard
Big Cats. – (Animal watch)
1.Big Cats – Juvenile literature
I.Title II.Orr, Richard
599.7'5

ISBN 1 84234 115 4

Printed and bound in Spain

ANIMAL WATCH

A Visual Introduction to

BIG CATS

Bernard Stonehouse

Illustrated by Richard Orr

CHERRYTREE BOOKS

PICTURE CREDITS

l = left, r = right, c = centre, t = top, b = bottom

BBC Natural History Unit Picture Library
Pages 9 b; 11 b; 13 r; 20 l; 29 b; 41 t; 43 b; 44 t; 45 c and bc

Frank Lane Picture Agency
Pages 14 b; 15 c; 31 b; 33 t; 35 b; 35 t; 38 b; 39 b; 44 tc

Natural History Photographic Agency
Pages 15 b; 17 r; 26 l; 29 r; 33 r; 40 b

Oxford Scientific Films
Pages 25 t, b; 31 t; 43 r; 44 b

Robert Harding Picture Library
Pages 17 b; 41 r; 44 tc

Topham Picturepoint
Pages 13 e; 23 r; 41 b

Woodfall Wild Images
Pages 19 r; 21 r; 29 t; 33 b; 37 b; 39 t; 45 t and tc

WorldSat
All satellite mapping

Additional artwork:
Martin Camm, cover, pages 8-9, 14-15, 38-39
Tim Haywood (Bernard Thornton Artists),
pages 12-13, 18-19, 40-41
Susanna Addario, pages 42-43

Art and editorial direction by **Peter Sackett**

Edited by **Norman Barrett**

Designed by **Paul Richards, Designers & Partners**

Picture research by **Lis Sackett**

CONTENTS

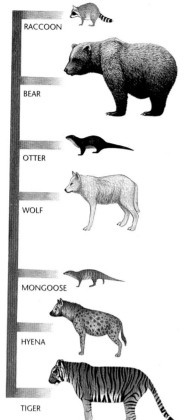

RACCOON

BEAR

OTTER

WOLF

MONGOOSE

HYENA

TIGER

INTRODUCING WILD CATS

Cats big and small are beautiful, graceful creatures, but they are also ferocious killers.

FAMILY TREE

Cats are mammals – warm-blooded animals that feed their young on milk. They belong to the order (major group) of mammals called Carnivora, which means 'meateaters'. Within the Carnivora, they belong to the suborder Fissipedia, meaning 'split-footed'. These include all the carnivores with separate toes in their feet. The other suborder is the Pinnipedia ('wing-footed', including the seals, sea-lions and walruses), in which the toes are bonded together to form flippers.

Other split-footed carnivores include raccoons (family Procyonidae), bears (Ursidae), otters, weasels, skunks and badgers (Mustelidae), dogs, foxes, wolves and jackals (Canidae), mongooses and civets (Viverridae), and hyenas (Hyaenidae). Cats are related to all these other meat-eating animals, perhaps most closely to the civets. But they are sufficiently different to make up a family of their own – the Felidae.

THE CATS ARE A FAMILY OF HUNTING animals, ranging in size from large (lions, tigers), through medium (ocelots, lynxes) to small (bobcats, domestic cats). They are graceful, sleek animals, with prominent ears, short noses and jaws, smooth fur, long legs, and usually a long, slender tail. Their feet are small and round, with sharp-pointed claws that in most species are retractile: they can be extended for scratching and holding, or pulled back into the foot for safety. A few cats have plain brown or black fur, but most are spotted or striped. This makes them very hard to see in dappled sunlight or against vegetation.

Like dogs, wolves, otters and some other members of the Carnivora, cats are adapted in shape and behaviour for hunting. Though some occasionally like to eat berries and fruit, they all live mostly by catching and eating other animals.

Tiger

Leopard

Jaguarundi

Jungle cat

Lynx

Clouded leopard

THE CAT FAMILY

The house cats that share our lives belong to a worldwide family of animals that includes lions, tigers, cheetahs and about 35 other living members. Biologists call the family the Felidae, from the Latin word *felis* for cat. House, or domestic, cats are among the smaller members of the family. It would take about 80 of them to outweigh a tiger. However, the felids are all very similar in skeleton, teeth and ways of hunting and living, so we call them all cats.

Cats of all kinds tend to live on their own or in small family groups. Except for the big cats of the African plains, they live quiet, hidden lives, usually keeping well away from people. Many are coloured to match their background, and are hard to see even when standing or lying close by.

CATS AND PEOPLE

Cats have always played an important role in human life, not only for their skins, but also because of their fierce nature. Many of the big cats, including lions, tigers and leopards, hunted and killed primitive humans, and scattered the farmers' cattle and sheep. Killing such an enemy with spear or catapult took far more skill and nerve than stalking buffalo, deer or antelope. Hunters came to think of the big cats as brave, fierce and clever. So the man who could kill one proved himself even braver, fiercer and cleverer.

Smaller cats such as cheetahs and caracals, caught as kittens and reared by hand, could be tamed and used to hunt other prey − a sport for kings and wealthy landowners. The smallest cats were kept around the farm and house, to catch rats and mice.

Serval

Jaguar

Cheetah

Lion

Wild cat

Ocelot

Where cats live

Cats live all over the temperate and tropical world. They inhabit a very wide range of environments throughout North and South America, Africa, Europe and Asia. Some species are adapted to life in forests, others to grasslands and open plains. A few live in hot deserts, and some on river banks and lake edges. There are none in the Arctic or Antarctic, but some live in the extreme cold of high mountain regions. Australia, New Zealand and New Guinea have no native cats. These islands were separated from the other continents before the first cats appeared. So, although cats were at different times able to spread freely from Asia to Europe, Africa and the Americas, they were never able to reach these outlying areas of the world.

ADAPTED FOR HUNTING

Although all cats are basically similar, their different shapes and sizes are suited for different methods of hunting, involving a wide range of prey. The big cats chase after large mammals such as deer and antelope. The smaller ones hunt squirrels, rats, mice, birds, insects and other small animals, usually by watching and pouncing.

Cats can run fast, leap, climb trees, hold their prey down with strong claws, and bite to kill with powerful jaws and sharp teeth. Behind their pointed canine teeth (the long, sharp ones on either side), are long cutting teeth called carnassials, which work together like shears or scissors to slice up the meat. Cats' stomachs produce powerful juices that digest meat quickly.

African lioness stalking in long grass

SERVAL

Order:	Meateaters (Carnivora)
Family:	Felidae
Subfamily:	Felinae
Latin name:	*Felis serval*
Colour:	Pale fawn or cream with large black bars and spots
Length:	Up to 1 m (3 ft 3 in), including tail
Weight:	Up to 10 kg (22 lb)
Habitat:	Grassland, semidesert, forest
Range:	Most of Africa south of the Sahara desert

BIG CATS AND SMALL

Tigers, the biggest of the family Felidae, measure up to 3 m (10 ft) from nose to tip of tail, and weigh up to 300 kg (660 lb). The black-footed cats of southern Africa, the smallest in the family, are less than 70 cm (28 in) long, and weigh less than 1.5 kg (3 lb 5 oz) − about half the weight of a house cat. The biggest tiger or lion today is not quite as big as some cave-living lions that existed up to about 15,000 years ago (see page 12). We know them only from bones, but they probably measured up to 4 m (13 ft) long, and weighed over 300 kg (660 lb).

Size is not the only difference between the subfamilies. There are smaller differences of anatomy and behaviour. For example, pantherines have a kind of voice-box that allows them to roar but not purr, while felines (such as house cats) can squeal and purr, but not roar.

Biologists cannot agree on which subfamily the cheetahs belong to, though they usually count as big cats. Nor can they agree on how the different species are grouped within the subfamilies. Some say that the 26 species of small cats differ enough to be placed in six or eight genera (subgroups). Others say they are similar enough to be grouped together in a single genus, *Felis.* That is how they are grouped in this book.

WHAT MAKES A CAT?

Different kinds of cats have different shapes and markings that suit them to their environment and way of life.

HOWEVER BIG OR SMALL, wherever you find them, the cats of the world share a strong family resemblance. Whether lions, cheetahs or house cats, they could not be anything else but cats. What are the features that make a cat? Look for:

- a round face with large, forward-looking eyes
- a short, snub nose, tipped with bare pink or black skin
- upright, pointed ears
- long whiskers growing from pads on either side of the nose
- long slender legs
- small round paws with sharp, retractile claws
- usually a long, flexible tail
- short fur, often spotted or striped

This particular cat is a serval, a tall, slender animal standing up to 50 cm (20 in) at the shoulder. Though obviously a cat, it has a relatively long neck, small head and enormous ears, and a short tail ringed with black stripes. Servals live in Africa, in a wide range of habitats from sparse, dry grassland to forest. The pale fawn or cream coat, marked with large black spots and stripes, makes servals almost invisible when they lie quietly in the shade. (See also pages 34-35.)

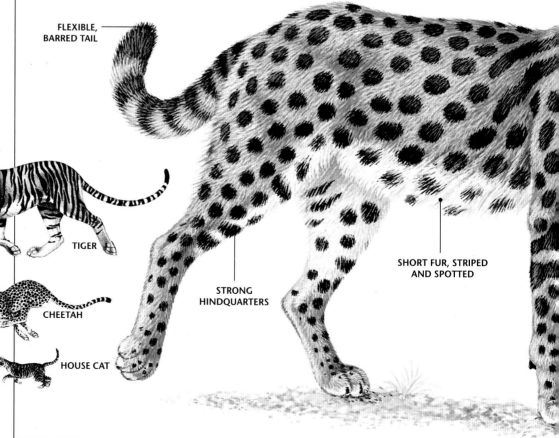

ERECT POINTED EARS

SHORT ROUND FACE

LARGE FORWARD – LOOKING EYES

SHARP CANINE TEETH

FLEXIBLE, BARRED TAIL

TIGER

CHEETAH

HOUSE CAT

STRONG HINDQUARTERS

SHORT FUR, STRIPED AND SPOTTED

Teeth and claws

TWO SUBFAMILIES

The family Felidae includes about 39 living species, or different kinds, of cats, together with many others known only as fossils.

Biologists divide the living species into two subfamilies, Pantherinae and Felinae:

■ the Pantherinae has 13 species, most of them 'big' cats weighing more than about 50 kg (110 lb)

■ the Felinae has 26 species, most of them small cats up to two or three times the weight of a house cat

Servals, shown here, are typical members of the subfamily Felinae, the small cats.

■ The cat's short nose and lower jaw are much shorter than a dog's. When hunting, cats rely less on scent, more on sight and hearing
■ The sharp canine teeth hold and pierce prey

■ The short jaw, with its scissor-blade back teeth, is a very efficient cutting mechanism
■ Massive jaw muscles under the skin create the typical round face
■ The tongue has a rough surface, useful for scraping meat from bones and grooming the fur
■ The whiskers are sensitive to wind currents and other small vibrations
■ The eyes have an internal reflective layer that makes the best use of dim light.
■ The pupils open wide in the dark, and close to a very small opening in bright light. Some cats, for example house cats, have pupils that reduce to slits. In others the pupils are always round.
■ The ears turn to detect and pinpoint very small sounds

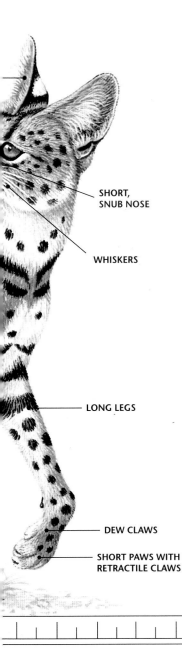

SHORT, SNUB NOSE

WHISKERS

LONG LEGS

DEW CLAWS

SHORT PAWS WITH RETRACTILE CLAWS

CATS' CLAWS

Cats walk on tip-toes. Their round paws are made up of just the tips of four fingers or toes. Thumbs are separate, on the inner sides of the legs. Called 'dew claws', they are useful in holding prey. Wrist and ankle bones make the legs longer, helping the cat to increase its stride and run faster.

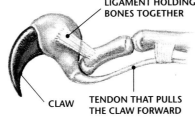

LIGAMENT HOLDING BONES TOGETHER

CLAW

TENDON THAT PULLS THE CLAW FORWARD

SUBSPECIES

Most species of cats live over wide geographical areas, and individuals of the same species differ from those in different populations. For example, the tigers found in different parts of eastern Asia differ in size, colour and other features. Biologists call these different groups subspecies, and add a third name to their 'official' Latin or Greek name. So all tigers are called *Panthera tigris,* but the big, pale-coloured Siberian ones belong to the subspecies *Panthera tigris altaica,* and the smaller ones of southern China to *Panthera tigris amoyensis.* Many such local subspecies, such as populations that used to live on the Indonesian islands of Bali (*Panthera tigris balica*) and Java (*Panthera tigris sondaica*), are now probably extinct.

Siberian tiger - one of several subspecies

LIONS

Once lions – the 'king of beasts' – were found all over Europe and Asia. Now these magnificent creatures are restricted to Africa and a small corner of India.

FACT FILE

Order:	Meateaters (Carnivora)
Family:	Felidae
Subfamily:	Pantherinae
Latin name:	*Panthera leo*
Colour:	Plain sandy brown; darker spots in cubs only
Length:	Average 2.7 m (9 ft)
Weight:	Up to 240 kg (530 lb)
Habitat:	Hot grassland and semidesert
Range:	Tropical Africa; Gir Sanctuary, Gujarat, India

RELATIONSHIPS

Lions first appear in the fossil record of northern Europe in rocks about 500,000 years old. They were larger than present-day lions, probably lived in caves, and were quite common, even as far north as Britain. In France and elsewhere, they often appear in cave drawings. At the same time, similar or smaller lions lived in Africa, the Middle East and India.

As civilization spread, lions disappeared. The last European lions died out about 2,000 years ago. They remained common in Asia until the 1800s, but systematic hunting in Arabia, Persia (modern Iran) and India destroyed most of them by the end of the century. Only about 100 survived in Asia, in a small patch of teak forest on the Kathiawar Peninsula of Gujarat, northwest India. This became the Gir Forest Wildlife Sanctuary, where about 200 Asian lions now live.

African lions are still plentiful, though many distinctive local populations (subspecies, see page 11) are now extinct. These include big Barbary lions of the North African Atlas Mountains and black-maned lions of Cape Province, South Africa.

LIONS LIVE IN ALL KINDS of tropical habitats, from thin forest to semidesert, but seem most at home in open grassland or savanna. Unlike other cats, they live in family groups, called 'prides'. The small pride shown here is made up of one adult male, three adult lionesses, and four cubs, two only a few weeks old, and two about a year old. Larger prides have more females and young.

Adult male lions are normally bigger and heavier than females, and their mane of long hair makes them look bigger still. One adult male dominates each pride, roaring, threatening and occasionally fighting to keep other males away. The prides stay together, moving slowly, week by week, around the large areas of open plain that are their feeding territories. They mark the territory boundaries with urine, the scent of which warns other lions to keep out. A typical territory contains herds of antelope, giraffes, buffalo, zebras and other grazing animals, which are the lions' main prey.

Living together protects the cubs and young lions from such predators as leopards, hyenas

The lion, symbol of strength

and jackals. Lionesses, which do most of the hunting, often hunt together more efficiently than they could on their own. They drive prey towards each other, combine to attack large animals, share their catches, and take joint care of the growing cubs.

Young males begin to grow a mane in their second or third year. About this time, they leave the pride in which they were reared, and set out on their own. Within two or three more years, the mane has developed fully and they have usually gathered a pride of their own.

FEEDING

Lions feed mainly on grazing mammals. They seldom hunt during the heat of the day. Instead they wander slowly after the herds, keeping close but not disturbing them, resting in the shade to save energy. Towards evening, two or three of the females set out to stalk, perhaps finding one antelope or zebra that is lagging behind the rest. Often working together, they move silently, keeping low until they have approached within a few metres. Then a final rush, a leap onto their victim's back, a fierce bite or a blow with a massive paw – and their prey lies dying. The male feeds first, then the females, then the young.

LAZY? FRIENDLY?

Lions never look at home on their own in zoo cages, but often live well in groups within game parks and safari parks. There are now many of these to be visited in Africa, Europe and elsewhere.

In parks or in the wild, take great care when you visit lions. They may remind you of your pet cat, looking lazy or even friendly. In fact they are dangerous. If you are in a car or truck, keep the windows up, and do not think for a moment of walking among them. Their 'laziness' is just to save energy, and they are not at all friendly to strangers. You might be surprised at how quickly they spring into action when they see supper approaching.

Where lions live

Practically all the world's wild lions live in Africa, south of the Sahara desert, mostly in open grassland and thin forest. Though their numbers are much reduced by hunting, they are still plentiful in national parks and reserves. Rangers and guides usually know where to find the prides from day to day, and will take visitors to them. The lions have grown used to people, and go about their business even with truckloads of visitors close by. Outside the parks, local people usually know where the local lions live, mainly so they can protect their cattle and keep out of their way.

Only one small population of Asian lions remains in the wild, in the Gir Forest, now part of a national park in Gujarat, northwest India. These, too, can be visited by organized groups of tourists.

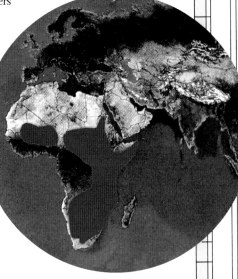

BREEDING

Female lions breed from their third or fourth year. When one is ready to mate, she releases a scent which stimulates the male to follow her. The male's attentions stimulate her ovaries to release tiny eggs into the oviducts, which are fertilized when the male injects sperm into her. Three or four fertilized eggs attach themselves to the wall of the uterus, where they develop into embryos.

These take about 17 weeks to grow to full size. Just before giving birth, the female leaves the pride and finds a safe, sheltered corner among rocks, or a cave or patch of dense grass. The cubs are born blind and helpless, weighing about 1.4 kg (3 lb). Their coats are spotted, making it harder for predators to find them.

The mother hunts to feed herself, leaving the cubs hidden. She carries them one by one in her mouth when she needs to move on. Feeding on her rich milk, they become lively and playful in three or four weeks. After six or seven weeks, they are big enough to join and run with the pride.

TIGERS

Striped hunter of Asia's forests and mountains, the tiger, largest of living cats, is ready to pounce on all kinds of unsuspecting prey.

FACT FILE

Order:	Meateaters (Carnivora)
Family:	Felidae
Subfamily:	Pantherinae
Latin name:	*Panthera tigris*
Colour:	Grey- to reddish-brown, paler underneath, strong black stripes
Length:	Up to 3 m (10 ft)
Weight:	Up to 300 kg (660 lb)
Habitat:	Hot grassland and semidesert
Range:	Eastern Asia including northeastern Siberia, China, India, Bangladesh, Nepal, Bhutan, Malay Peninsula, Thailand, Java, Sumatra

SAVING THE TIGER

In 1972, the World Wildlife Fund launched 'Operation Tiger', a major campaign to protect all eight subspecies of tigers. Estimates had shown that the number of tigers had dropped from about 100,000 in 1920 to 30,000 by 1960, and under 5,000 by 1970. The decline affected every subspecies, some to the point of extinction. WWF continue helping to provide reserves and protection for many populations of tigers. The total in the late 1990s was estimated at between 5,000 and 7,000.

Siberian tiger in the snow

TIGERS, EVEN MORE than lions, are everyone's idea of wild, fierce animals, cunning, clever and untamable. They are versatile hunters that live by their wits. More lively and active than lions, they stalk and pounce on a much wider range of prey.

Like lions, they lie up during the heat of the day, hunting mostly in the cool of the evening or at night. Young tigers learn the tricks of hunting from their mothers during their first two or three years of life. Fully grown, they move fast enough to chase forest pigs, with power and strength to bite and break the necks of antelopes and other large grazers. They wait patiently for monkeys to come within reach, leaping 4 m (13 ft) or more to knock them from trees. They catch birds on the wing, and scoop fish and turtles from rivers with their paws. Some learn to grab porcupines without getting a mouthful of sharp quills.

Tigers are in many ways more intelligent than lions, and easier to tame, at least as cubs. Taken young, they were given by ancient kings as presents to each other. Modern biologists who have hand-reared them find them splendid pets until almost fully grown, but unreliable or dangerous as they grow older.

Tigers in the world live very much on their own, each adult owning a territory or range which it patrols and marks with urine. Where there is plenty of food, territories are just a

Indian tiger running through grass

few kilometres across, and can be patrolled in a day. Where food is scarcer, the range may be as much as 60 km (37 miles) wide and twice as long, taking several days or weeks to patrol. When territories overlap, as they often seem to, neighbouring animals do not fight. They keep out of each others' way, except occasionally to share kills.

Wherever they live, few natural enemies are capable of harming tigers. Their only serious enemy is man.

BREEDING

Tigers and tigresses come together only when the females are ready to mate. They keep company for one or two weeks. After a gestation period of about 16 weeks, the mother produces three to four cubs, each weighing up to 1.5 kg (3 lb 3 oz). The cubs are striped from birth. After feeding on their mother's milk for about 6 weeks, they begin to take meat, which the mother brings to them. At 12 weeks, they are tumbling, playful cubs, following their mother and investigating the exciting world around them. At six or seven months, they join her in hunting. This can be a hard school, in which only half the cubs survive. After two years, those still living are ready to strike out on their own. By three years, they are fully grown. Tigresses probably breed every third or fourth year.

RELATIONSHIPS

Lions and tigers, the two biggest living cats, are more closely related than they first look. It is difficult to tell some of their bones apart. Even their skulls are very similar, and fossil bones are even harder to distinguish than modern ones. Though they are unlikely to meet in the wild, in zoos they interbreed successfully (see below right).

Lion

Tiger

The most obvious differences between the two species, notably in colour and shape, arise from their different ways of life. Lions live mainly on open, dusty plains, while tigers live mainly in forests and dense grasslands. Tigers are found over a very wide geographical range, from the hot rainforests of central India to the cool mountain forests of Siberia. Eight local subspecies have been described, based chiefly on differences in colour and patterns of stripes. Sadly, three of them are extinct and three more are very close to extinction.

Sumatran

Siberian

Patterns of stripes on Sumatran and Siberian tigers

Where tigers live

Within historic times, tigers were plentiful in forested areas from Turkey in the east, along the southern shores of the Caspian Sea, through Iran, Afghanistan and India to Burma (Myanmar), Sumatra, Java and Bali in Southeast Asia, and across central China north to Manchuria and Siberia. Within many of these areas the tigers retreated as their forests were cleared for farming and timber. In the last hundred years, thousands were shot for sport, to protect sheep, cattle and villagers, and for their magnificent skins and other body parts. Now there are relatively few tigers left in any part of their range.

Some subspecies are extinct, or have living representatives only in zoos. You can see wild tigers in some of the Indian game parks and reserves, and half-wild ones in American and European safari parks, where they often seem to live happily.

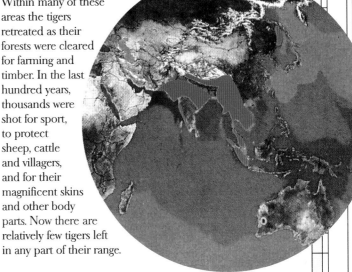

LIGERS, TIGONS AND LEOPONS

Lions and tigers that are well looked after breed quite readily in zoos and game parks. That the two species are closely related is shown by the ease with which they interbreed. In zoos where there were only one or two of each, they have been found to interbreed freely, producing cubs with an assortment of colours and stripes. The cub of a lion and a tigress is called a 'liger'. One from a tiger and lioness is a 'tigon'. Both ligers and tigons have been reared to full maturity. Though not all are fertile (able to produce offspring), one at least was mated successfully with a lion. Lions and leopards (pages 16-17), too, have been crossbred, producing 'leopons'.

LEOPARDS

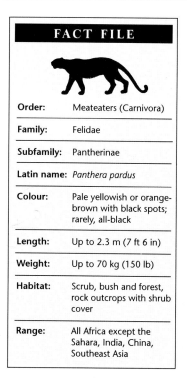

Now you see them, now you don't. Spotted leopards wait silent and still on the forest edge until they are ready to strike.

FACT FILE

Order:	Meateaters (Carnivora)
Family:	Felidae
Subfamily:	Pantherinae
Latin name:	*Panthera pardus*
Colour:	Pale yellowish or orange-brown with black spots; rarely, all-black
Length:	Up to 2.3 m (7 ft 6 in)
Weight:	Up to 70 kg (150 lb)
Habitat:	Scrub, bush and forest, rock outcrops with shrub cover
Range:	All Africa except the Sahara, India, China, Southeast Asia

RELATIONSHIPS

Leopards are lightweight cousins of lions and tigers. They are more slender in build, more agile and flexible in movement. Noticeably smaller than their cousins, with shorter legs, they have a proportionately longer tail and smaller head. The face is broad, the ears are small, round, and spaced far apart. They have big, well-padded paws, with sharp claws that help them to hold prey and to climb. While fully grown lions and tigers become too heavy to shin up trees, leopards remain lithe and active throughout their lives.

Their most striking difference is their pattern of spots. Lions are plain-coloured, tigers are striped, while leopards are spotted. The spots are single, or grouped in tight rings, or 'rosettes', of two, three or four (see 'Leopard spots' on page 17), making an all-over pattern from the broad forehead to the tip of the long, swishing tail.

Another name for the leopard is 'panther'. This can be used for any leopard, but is most often given to very dark brown or even black ones. These are not a different species – just unusually dark individuals that appear occasionally among litters of normal colour. While real 'black panthers' are very black, you sometimes see dark brown ones with typical black spots showing through.

IF YOU ARE WALKING through country where leopards are plentiful, keep looking upwards. If they are hiding in the long grass, you are unlikely to see them at all. Look instead at rock ledges and the lower branches of trees. Look very carefully, because there is no animal more difficult to spot on a hot, sunny afternoon than a resting leopard.

Though similar in background colour to lions and tigers, leopards have spots rather than stripes for their camouflage markings. When they are lying in shade during the heat of the day, the spots make them almost invisible. In the half-light of evening, when leopards wake up and start to hunt, again they blend remarkably with their dappled background.

Leopards live and walk alone, usually silent and almost invisible. They lie low by day, and are most active in the evenings and early mornings when their prey is about. You will seldom see a leopard moving under a hot sun. More often they choose a place of safety in the shade, where they can sleep, and watch, and sleep again without being disturbed.

In the evenings they become hunters. They wake up, yawn, stretch, and sharpen their claws on the nearest branch or tree stump. Then they keep watch for the smaller mammals that are their main prey – often deer, antelopes or

Where leopards live

Leopard on the lookout for prey

monkeys. Having spotted a victim, they slip quietly down to the ground, stalk silently on tip-toe, then strike hard, pinning down their prey with teeth and claws. Sometimes they wait in their tree, ready to pounce or drop on animals walking beneath.

Leopards have long canine teeth in the front of their jaws, strong enough to tear through tough hides. On either side are sharp, 'carnassials', teeth like shears, capable of cutting meat to ribbons. After a first feed, they often drag away what is left of the carcase, hiding it among rocks or under bushes.

Sometimes they climb with it back into their tree, draping it among the lower branches where it will be safe from other predators.

Leopards like to live in thin forest, grassland or scrub, avoiding only the driest deserts, where there is little food for them.

Apart from the Sahara Desert, they live all over Africa, from the Atlas Mountains in the north to the southern tip,

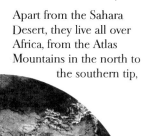

and throughout southern Asia from Turkey to India, Indo-China, China, Malaysia and the Koreas. The spread of humans has reduced their numbers, so they are nowhere very plentiful.

They are often hunted, some because they kill farm animals, others just for their beautiful skins. As a result, they are becoming scarcer.

Today you are most likely to see leopards in game reserves and other protected areas, where they are safe from poachers. Game wardens often know where to find them – but they are shy animals, and you still have to look very carefully to see one.

BREEDING

Leopards live and hunt alone. You seldom see more than one at a time, except when they are about to breed. Each leopard has its own home range or hunting area, which may overlap with ranges of several other leopards. The scent of their urine marks the ranges, so each leopard knows when others are about. When a female is ready to mate, the scent of her urine changes, becoming a signal for neighbouring males. She may mate with several, and then leave them to carry on hunting alone.

After a gestation period of 13 weeks the mother produces from one to four kittens, hiding them away in a quiet, sheltered corner between rocks or under bushes. There she feeds them, first on her own milk, later on meat

that she brings into the den. Only if there is plenty of food will she raise as many as four. More often the smallest and weakest members of the litter die, leaving more food for the one or two survivors.

Black leopard, also called panther

LEOPARD SPOTS

Hold the tips of your thumb and three of your fingers together, spaced slightly apart. Dip them in soot or black paint, and dab them repeatedly on a yellow-brown background, sometimes just one, two or three tips, sometimes all four together. That is the kind of spotting that you see on a leopard. Against a plain background – as you might find in a zoo enclosure or cage – a spotted leopard stands out a mile. You might wonder how an animal so vividly patterned could possibly hide. But among the branches of a leafy tree, in dappled bright sunlight and dark shade, a leopard simply disappears.

SNOW LEOPARDS, CLOUDED LEOPARDS AND MARBLED CATS

FACT FILE

SNOW LEOPARD (OUNCE)

Order:	Meateaters (Carnivora)
Family:	Felidae
Subfamily:	Pantherinae
Latin name:	*Panthera uncia*
Colour:	White and yellow with black spots and stripes
Length:	Up to 2.3 m (7 ft 6 in)
Weight:	Unrecorded
Habitat:	Mountain slopes up to about 3000 m (10,000 ft)
Range:	Mountain regions of southern Russia, Tibet and other parts of China

CLOUDED LEOPARD

Order:	Meateaters (Carnivora)
Family:	Felidae
Subfamily:	Pantherinae
Latin name:	*Neofelis nebulosa*
Colour:	Tan or yellow with black spots and stripes; white underneath
Length:	2 m (6 ft 6 in)
Weight:	20 kg (45 lb)
Habitat:	Dense tropical forest
Range:	Nepal, southern China, Malaysia, Sumatra, Borneo

MARBLED CAT

Order:	Meateaters (Carnivora)
Family:	Felidae
Subfamily:	Pantherinae
Latin name:	*Pardofelis marmorata*
Colour:	Tan with darker brown blotches, ringed and spotted with black
Length:	1 m (3 ft 3 in)
Weight:	About 5 kg (11 lb)
Habitat:	Dense mountain forest
Range:	Nepal, Burma, Malaysia, Indonesia

NONE OF THESE THREE KINDS of leopard-like cats is closely related to true leopards (pages 16-17), but all are similar in colour, markings and ways of life.

Of the three, snow leopards (also called ounces) come closest to true leopards in size, colour and markings. They stand almost as tall as a leopard, but are more slender in build, with a proportionately longer tail. The most obvious difference, indeed the most striking feature of these animals, is their lovely dense fur, which makes them seem larger and more chunky than they really are, with thick legs and tail.

Snow leopards live in high mountain regions of central Asia, which may be hot in summer but intensely cold and snow-covered in winter. Even in summer they need a dense coat, for the air chills as soon as the sun goes down, and nights can be cold and windy. For winter they grow an especially thick coat, 5–10 cm (2–4 in) long over most of the body.

Each snow leopard has its own territory, often of several square kilometres, in which it lives and hunts. Their food is mainly small birds and mammals, ranging in size from mice to mountain goats, which they stalk among the rocks and bushes. Snow leopards mate in late summer and produce litters of two or three kittens in spring.

Where they live

Clouded leopard on the prowl

Snow leopards live mostly in wild country far from human settlements, and are not known to attack humans. However, they may become a nuisance by taking sheep and goats.

'Ounce', the old name for snow leopards, is not often used today.

Snow leopards

Snow leopards used to live in the mountain ranges from Iran in the west to southern China in the east, including southern Russia and Tibet. These are wild places, where it is almost impossible to count animals or estimate their numbers. So we do not know how many snow leopards there were in the past, or how many there are now. But we know that many thousands have been shot for their fur, probably more than are being born and reared, so their numbers are likely to have fallen and their range decreased.

Clouded leopards and marbled cats live in the forests of Nepal, northern India, Burma, Malaysia, Indonesia and southern China. These too are areas where it is difficult to estimate numbers, so we do not know how many there are. But again both species are hunted for their fur. And in many of their homelands, huge areas of forest are being cut down for timber. This brings work and money to the people who live there, but destroys the forest, and may make it more difficult for these beautiful cats to survive.

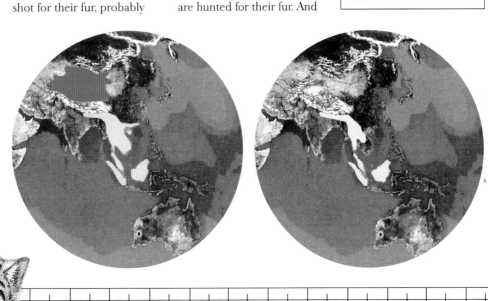

	Snow leopard
	Clouded leopard
	Marbled cat

FOREST CATS

Clouded leopards are smaller than snow leopards, and marbled cats are much smaller still, about as big as a good-sized domestic cat. Their markings are rather similar, including both spots and rosettes, and also patches of darker fur edged with black – a pattern that you sometimes see in marble.

These are both species of Asian tropical forests, slender and lithe enough to climb trees, where they spend much of their time. They probably find it easier to live among the branches than on the damp and rather dark jungle floor, though they come down to ground level to hunt in clearings and along river banks.

Neither species is common and we do not know much about how they live. Both feed mainly on birds, monkeys and other small mammals, and tree-living lizards. They tend to keep away from people, though clouded leopards occasionally attack sheep, chickens and other domestic animals close to villages. Both are hunted for their fur, and both lose their homes when their forests are cut down for timber.

Marbled cat

Clouded leopard

LYNXES OF THE OLD WORLD

Lynxes and their caracal cousins can be distinguished from other cats by their tufted ears and short tails.

FACT FILE

EURASIAN LYNX

Order:	Meateaters (Carnivora)
Family:	Felidae
Subfamily:	Pantherinae
Latin name:	*Lynx lynx*
Colour:	Yellow-brown with grey-black spots
Length:	1.2 m (4 ft)
Weight:	25 kg (55 lb)
Habitat:	Temperate forests
Range:	Scandinavia, Balkans, Spain, eastern Europe, Siberia, northern China, Middle East, Turkey

CARACAL (DESERT LYNX)

Order:	Meateaters (Carnivora)
Family:	Felidae
Subfamily:	Pantherinae
Latin name:	*Lynx caracal*
Colour:	Reddish brown, pale underneath, dark ears, eyebrows and nose
Length:	75 cm (2 ft 6 in)
Weight:	16 kg (35 lb)
Habitat:	Desert and dry grassland
Range:	Most of Africa and the Middle East, southern Russia, India

RELATIONSHIPS

Lynxes are medium-sized cats with sturdy bodies and short tails. The character that distinguishes them from other cats is their long ears, with tufts of fur on the tips that make them look even longer. They are found mainly in temperate forest and deserts in both the 'Old World' and the 'New World' (see page 21). Old-World forms include true lynxes, which range widely from Spain to Siberia, and the smaller but closely related caracals, which live in semideserts of Africa, Turkey and India. For the New World forms, see pages 22-23.

LYNXES ARE STRONGLY BUILT CATS of medium size, with stocky, muscular bodies, short, powerful legs, and curiously stumpy tails. Many have long, luxurious fur, especially in winter. In colour they vary from pale to dark tawny-brown, and the amount and strength of spotting varies in different localities. Spanish lynxes have the darkest spots, and some biologists think they are different enough to be a separate species.

Long fur lines the chin, making the face look almost square. The long, tufted ears, usually darker than the rest of the head, stand upright when the lynx is hunting. As in most other cats, the sexes are similar.

Lynxes live mainly in old, mature forests, where natural clearings, fallen trees and dense undergrowth provide a wide range of hunting grounds and choice of food. They can survive in plantations and along the forest edge, and in dry parts of their range may live among shrubs and bushes. They hunt by stalking and pouncing, mostly in the evenings and early mornings.

Deer, rabbits and other small mammals are their main food, but they catch birds when they can, and enter streams to catch fish.

Caracals, similar in shape to lynxes, are smaller and generally thinner, with reddish, unspotted coats. The tail is longer and the legs more slender. Caracals are built for speed and agility, rather than strength. Like lynxes they range widely across the Old World, throughout Africa and across southern Asia, but they live in desert, scrub or grassland rather than forest. They run fast enough to catch hares or antelope, and can leap a metre or two to catch low-flying birds.

Both lynxes and caracals produce litters of two or three kittens, which they hide away in undergrowth to protect from predators.

Lynx emerging from the forest

Eurasian lynx

OLD WORLD, NEW WORLD

'Old World' is the name given to the big continental mass of Europe, Asia and Africa, contrasting it with the 'New World' of North and South America. People who emigrated from Europe to North America in the 1800s spoke of leaving to find 'a new life in a new world', and the names have stuck.

Of course the Americas are just as old as Europe, Asia and Africa. Many millions of years ago they were together in one great landmass, which we have called Gondwana, and animals – then mainly reptiles – could roam freely from one side to the other. Then Gondwana split, forming the two landmasses, and the great basin between them that is now the

Atlantic Ocean. Land animals could no longer wander between the two, and each landmass developed its own kinds of birds and mammals.

There was some mixing later when, for a few million years, a broad pathway

Caracal

of dry land existed at the northern end of the Pacific Ocean, now the Bering Strait. Some mammals that had evolved in Asia were able to cross into North America along this route (called the Bering Bridge), and vice versa. Then the sea level rose and the 'bridge' between the two was closed. So there are lions and tigers in the Old World but not in the New, jaguars in the New World but not in the Old – and different but similar kinds of lynxes in both.

Close-up of a caracal

Where they live

Before humans evolved, Old World lynxes lived in the huge forests that covered most of Europe, through Turkey to Russia, and across Siberia to the Kamchatka Peninsula and northern China. As the forests were destroyed to make way for farms, villages and towns, lynxes gradually lost ground. Farmers trapped and shot them, reducing their numbers further.

Today there are only a few remnants left in western Europe, in forested corners of the Spanish and French Pyrenees, Austria and northern Scandinavia. There are more of them in eastern Europe, from the Baltic Sea to Romania and Greece, and in wild forest areas from southern Russia to Tibet, Mongolia, Manchuria and Siberia.

Caracals range through dry forests, scrub, grasslands and semideserts of Africa, from the Cape of Good Hope to Morocco, and in similar habitats from Turkey to India. Nowhere are they plentiful. Like lynxes, they hunt mainly at twilight.

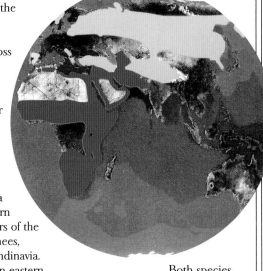

Both species are shy and hard for visitors to see. Your best chances are in a reserve or park, and you need to find local guides or rangers who can tell you exactly where to look. Even then you will have to be patient, and perhaps lucky as well.

	Eurasian lynx
	Caracal

CARACALS

Found by hunters, caracal kittens have often been tamed and trained to hunt singly or in groups. Never especially friendly as

pets, they are kept mainly to show off their skills at catching birds and running down small mammals.

LYNXES OF THE NEW WORLD

Lynxes and bobcats once ranged widely in North and Central America, but now they are safe only in wilderness areas.

FACT FILE

NORTH AMERICAN LYNX

Order:	Meateaters (Carnivora)
Family:	Felidae
Subfamily:	Pantherinae
Latin name:	*Lynx canadensis*
Colour:	Yellow-brown with grey-black spots
Length:	1.2 m (4 ft)
Weight:	25 kg (55 lb)
Habitat:	Temperate forests
Range:	Alaska, Canada and northern USA

BOBCAT

Order:	Meateaters (Carnivora)
Family:	Felidae
Subfamily:	Pantherinae
Latin name:	*Lynx rufus*
Colour:	Tawny brown, with irregular dark patches and spots
Length:	90 cm (3 ft)
Weight:	Up to 8 kg (18 lb)
Habitat:	Forest, woodland, scrub, grassland, semidesert
Range:	United States, western and eastern Canada, Mexico

RELATIONSHIPS

New World lynxes of Canada, the United States and Mexico are similar to and closely related to Old World lynxes (pages 20-21), so much so that some biologists regard them as different races (subspecies) of the same species. Others say that, as they have lived in different parts of the world for thousands of years, with no possibility of interbreeding, it is better to regard them as separate species and give them separate names. Bobcats, though quite like North American lynxes in some ways, are much smaller, with a different way of life, and are certainly different enough to form a species of their own.

NORTH AMERICAN LYNXES are similar in almost every way to those of Europe and Asia. Their ancestors are thought to have crossed from northeastern Asia to North America during the Ice Age, when the sea level was lower and dry land extended where there is now the Bering Strait. The new arrivals found forests with conditions similar to those they had left behind, and continued living much as they had lived in their old homeland. There was little need for them to change, so the lynxes in both parts of the world have remained very similar.

In North America, lynxes are found throughout the extensive lowland and low mountain forests, woodlands and scrub-covered plains. They live mainly on hares, rabbits and other small mammals, and birds. In the mountains they take mountain sheep and goats, dropping on them from above like leopards, or running them down in a chase. They hunt by day and in the evenings.

Human settlers who cleared the forests regarded lynxes as enemies because they took their sheep, goats and chickens. The lynxes retreated into the remaining forests, where hunters and trappers pursued them for their skins. Today they thrive best in the wild areas where, despite continued hunting, they are still quite plentiful.

Bobcats are the smaller cats of American woodlands and plains. Looking rather like big domestic cats, they are noticeably more slender than North American lynxes and weigh only about one-third as much. The ears are less sharply tufted, the coats more delicately spotted and striped, with prominent dark stripes on either side of the face. The tails are shorter, often with a black tufted tip.

North American lynx

Where they live

They live generally on more open ground than lynxes, feeding on smaller prey which they hunt by stalking and pouncing. More agile than lynxes, they shin up trees and scramble among rocks after their prey. Everyday diet includes mice, rats, squirrels, chipmunks, rabbits and hares, but bobcats have been known also to eat tortoises, deer and sheep. Despite their usefulness in killing rodents, farmers have tended to hunt them mercilessly. As a result, like their larger cousins the lynxes, bobcats are most plentiful in the wilder areas.

Bobcats

BREEDING

Lynxes live solitary lives, each adult patrolling an extensive territory and only occasionally meeting or mixing with others. They mate in February or March, and the babies (called kittens or cubs) are born about 10 weeks later, usually in litters of two or three. Kept safe and dry in a hollow tree or cave, the kittens feed on their mother's milk for four or five months, but after the first month are fed also on meat that the mother brings home from her hunting trips.

Bobcats mate in spring and produce litters of three or four kittens some seven weeks later. The kittens feed on milk for two or three months, then begin to follow their mothers on hunting expeditions close to the home den. They reach independence at eight or nine months, when they set off on a long journey, possibly more than 160 km (100 miles), to find territories of their own.

North American lynxes lived originally in all the forested areas of North America, from Alaska and Labrador in the north, throughout Canada, to the southern United States. They remain widespread in Alaska and Canada, but have disappeared from all but the wilder parts of the northern United States. Bobcats are still plentiful throughout the United States, southwestern Canada and northern Mexico, though they too are restricted to the wilder areas in some of the more heavily populated southern states.

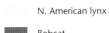

N. American lynx

Bobcat

Canadian bobcat

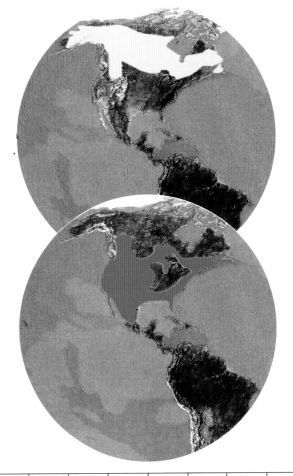

VARYING HARES AND LYNXES

North Canadian woodlands are the home of varying hares, so-called because their fur changes colour from grey-brown in summer to white in winter. Summer and winter alike, these are the main prey of North American lynxes. Throughout the 1800s, both hares and lynxes were trapped for their furs, which were sold by the thousand to the Canadian Hudson Bay Company.

Scientists examining the company records found that the numbers of skins bought from year to year differed greatly. In some years both species were plentiful, but in others both were scarce. This indicated that numbers of one depended on numbers of the other.

Over each period of 9 or 10 years, numbers of hares rose steadily, showing that they were breeding faster than the lynxes could eat them. Then they suddenly became scarce, probably because they had eaten out all the vegetation, and there were fewer around to catch. When this happened, numbers of lynxes also dropped

dramatically, because now there were few hares left to feed on, and the lynxes were starving. Then numbers of hares would increase again, and numbers of lynxes gradually follow. In this way, the historic records of a company helped to show how the lives of two species are closely interlinked.

JAGUARS

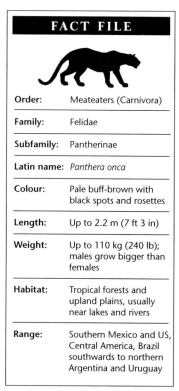

Biggest of the American cats, jaguars are the hunters of the tropical forests. Their beautiful spotted coats make them hard to see against the leafy background.

FACT FILE

Order:	Meateaters (Carnivora)
Family:	Felidae
Subfamily:	Pantherinae
Latin name:	*Panthera onca*
Colour:	Pale buff-brown with black spots and rosettes
Length:	Up to 2.2 m (7 ft 3 in)
Weight:	Up to 110 kg (240 lb); males grow bigger than females
Habitat:	Tropical forests and upland plains, usually near lakes and rivers
Range:	Southern Mexico and US, Central America, Brazil southwards to northern Argentina and Uruguay

RELATIONSHIPS

The name 'jaguar' comes from a South American native word meaning 'dog'. The local Spanish name throughout their range is 'tigre', or tiger, and Brazilians call them 'onça', or 'ounce', which is an alternative name for snow leopards (pages 18-19). However, jaguars are neither dogs, tigers nor leopards. They are large spotted cats of South America, and by far the largest of the New World cats.

They are if anything the South American equivalent of Old World leopards, though more heavily built. The biggest jaguars, living at the southern end of their range in Argentina, stand almost as tall as tigers, but are lighter in weight. Those from Mexico and Central America are much smaller, closer in size to leopards or large lynxes. Though most jaguars are spotted, a few are dark brown or almost black.

Despite these differences, biologist agree that there is only one species of jaguar. Some say that, because of the differing sizes and colours, we should divide them into at least a dozen subspecies. In this book, we treat them all as a single, undivided species.

WITH ITS ROUND EARS, long tail, tawny skin and all-over pattern of black spots, a jaguar at first glance looks very much like a leopard. But look again: the body is thicker and more clumsy, the face is broader, shorter and usually darker, and many of the spots are arranged in rings with a dark spot in the middle.

Jaguars may well be descended from leopards that, 10,000 or more years ago, invaded North America from the Old World via the Bering Bridge (see page 21). Conditions in the New World were slightly different for them, and they evolved into slightly different animals.

Fossil skulls and other bones show that several different kinds of jaguar-like animals have lived in North America, including some that were much larger and heavier than those of today.

The modern kind of jaguar, too, once ranged more widely across North America, in the end retreating as humans began to spread.

Today jaguars are found in forests and marshlands, usually far from people, often close to rivers or running water. They swim well and, unlike most other cats, seem to enjoy splashing and keeping cool in water. Young jaguars climb trees, sometimes hunting for birds and mammals in the branches. Older ones become heavy and less willing to climb, and hunt mainly on the ground.

Jaguars live singly, patrolling large territories in a constant search for food. They come together only for mating. They can run fast, but only in short sprints.

When hunting, they pad silently along trails through the forest or long grass, 'freezing' at the sight of prey, then stalking, crouching and finally springing.

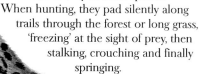

BREEDING

Like most other cats, jaguars live alone for most of their lives, patrolling large territories and keeping out of each other's way. When a female is ready to breed, her scent changes to attract males from neighbouring territories. Sometimes as many as six or seven will follow her, fighting among themselves and answering her noisy calls.

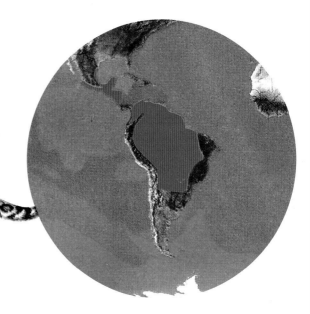

Jaguar scratching log

Ground-living mammals are their main prey, including wild pigs, capybara (rodents that look like large guinea-pigs), rats, porcupines, deer, armadillos and, occasionally, mountain sheep. With their powerful jaws and unusually large canine teeth, they can crunch through the shells of river turtles or snap off the heads of snakes at a single bite.

In the 1800s, when immigrant farmers from Europe brought in sheep, cattle and horses, jaguars emerged from the forests to hunt these new forms of prey. A large jaguar can bring down a sheep, foal or calf with ease, and may tackle even a fully grown steer or horse. Farmers waged war against them, driving them back into the forests and reducing their numbers. The skins they collected sold well, creating a demand in world markets, and making it worth while to kill every jaguar that appeared.

After mating with one or several of them, she becomes pregnant. About 14 weeks later she produces up to four kittens, hiding them deep in the forest. For three or four weeks they feed only on her milk. Then she brings meat back to the den, and after seven or eight weeks the kittens hunt with her. Young jaguars stay with their mothers for a year or more, before wandering off to find territories of their own.

Where jaguars live

Though once quite common, jaguars are rarely seen today in the southern forests of Mexico. There may still be more of them than we know in remote mountain areas. They are most commonly found in the forests of Central America, Colombia, Bolivia, Peru, Ecuador, Venezuela and central Brazil, reaching their southern limits in northern Argentina, Paraguay and possibly Uruguay. In southern Belize, a large area of forest has been set aside as a reserve for studying jaguars in the wild.

DANGEROUS TO HUMANS

Jaguars have good reason to keep out of the way of humans. Wherever they make themselves known, they tend to be shot, because people judge them to be dangerous. A jaguar that leaves the safety of the forest and visits farms or settlements may well be hungry, and there are plenty of records of jaguars killing cattle, sheep and people – enough to make us wary of them.

However, the wanderer may just be a young animal that cannot find room to establish a feeding territory of its own among the trees. Sadly, it is unlikely to find its way back to the forest before someone shoots it. Whether dangerous or not, jaguars have furs that are much in demand for fashion clothing, and no peasant farmer with a gun can afford to let one escape.

Jaguar skins help poor farmers make a living

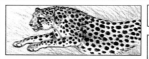

CHEETAHS

These long-legged hunting cats of Africa and the Middle East are the fastest animals on four legs.

FACT FILE

Order:	Meateaters (Carnivora)
Family:	Felidae
Subfamily:	Pantherinae
Latin name:	*Acinonyx jubatus*
Colour:	Tawny yellow with black spots
Length:	2 m (6 ft 6 in)
Weight:	Up to 65 kg (145 lb)
Habitat:	Grassland, desert scrub, thin woodland
Range:	Africa, western Asia

TIGER

CHEETAH

HOUSE CAT

RELATIONSHIPS

Nobody can doubt that cheetahs are cats, members of the family Felidae. But biologists have never been able to decide which of the two subfamilies of cats – the lions and tigers (Pantherinae) or the smaller cats (Felinae) – they belong to.

If size were all that mattered, they would be grouped with the lions and tigers. But there are other differences to be considered. Cheetahs cannot roar or even growl. Instead they scream, miaow and purr like small cats. They are different, too, from all other cats in having claws that stick out all the time and are never pulled back into a sheath. This is connected with their great speed, for the claws give good grip – just like an athlete's spiked running shoes.

It may be that cheetahs are neither pantherines nor felines, but rate a subfamily of their own. In this book, they are included with the big cats, which they seem to match better.

More than any other cats, the cheetah is built for speed. With its long slender limbs and tail, and lithe, muscular body, in a chase across the plains a cheetah can outrun and outmanoeuvre all but the fastest antelopes and gazelles. It is not surprising that these wonderful animals have for long been admired and cherished by man for their hunting skills.

Cheetahs stand and sit tall, looking very much like thin, long-legged leopards. The coat is basically tawny, paler underneath from chin to tail, with an overall pattern of large, single black spots. The tail is long – sometimes half as long as the body. The head is small and broad, with round ears. There is a dark stripe from eye to chin on either side of the muzzle. The chest is deep, the rear half of the body slender, and the hind legs packed with muscles – the mainsprings that drive the animal forward when it starts to run.

The long legs and flexible spine combine to provide the enormously long stride that is the secret of the cheetah's speed. From a standing start, cheetahs can reach 80 km/h (50 mph) in a few seconds, but they tire very quickly.

Adult cheetahs seldom travel or hunt together, but seem to be very much aware of each other on their open plains. Each cheetah needs 8–10 sq km (3-4 sq miles) of good grassland to live in, even more in dry areas

Cheetah watching for prey

Where cheetahs live

when there are fewer prey animals about. They hunt mainly in the daytime. A hungry cheetah sits upright on a high point, scanning the ground below and sniffing the wind.

On sighting prey, a cheetah walks to within a few hundred metres, then starts running, choosing one from a group and pursuing it until it falls. Small antelopes and gazelles, young hartebeest, zebra foals, bushbuck (type of antelope) and even hares are taken, along with any birds that are unwary enough to be caught.

CHEETAH ON A LEAD

In several parts of their range from India to eastern Africa, cheetahs have been caught and reared in captivity. Surprisingly for such lively animals, they respond well to handling, and seem perfectly happy in captivity –

just so long as they are let out to hunt from time to time. During the Middle Ages, pairs of cheetahs trained to hunt and retrieve were shipped to Europe, to be prized by emperors in their courts. Sometimes, packs of a dozen or more, trained to hunt together, were turned loose on herds of grazing animals to show off their skills at killing.

Cheetahs live mainly in the dry grasslands and semidesert areas of Africa and western Asia. They have never been plentiful in any of their haunts, or so conspicuous as lions and other large mammals. So seeing just a few on a long safari might mean that they were flourishing, not dying out.

However, although catching them to be trained as hunting animals (see left) did not drastically reduce them, in recent times their numbers have fallen heavily through hunting for their beautiful fur.

Less than 100 years ago they were found all over Africa except in the rainforests. Now hunting has eliminated them from Cape Province, Natal and other well-farmed areas, but they are still present in scattered populations from Mozambique and Namibia, north to Eritrea in the east and Morocco in the west.

They were once widespread across southwestern Asia, from Turkey to central India, even in the recent past. Now there are only thin remnant populations in Arabia, Turkmenistan, Afghanistan and western India.

The best places to see cheetahs today are probably Kenya's wildlife parks. There they are as plentiful as you will find anywhere, and many are quite used to being watched and photographed by visitors.

BREEDING

Females that are ready to mate select one or more partners and stay with them for two or three weeks. If there are several males, each tries to guard her jealously from the others, and there are often quarrels. She becomes pregnant, and produces her litter of three to six kittens some 13 weeks later. The kittens stay in a den for several weeks. By the time they emerge, one or two will be fatter and bigger than the others, and these are the most likely to survive. Usually up to half the kittens in any litter die before they are a year old.

Those that do survive follow their mother closely, standing by while she kills, then moving in to share the feast. By the time they

are half-grown, they may be joining in the hunt themselves. Mother cheetahs guard their young fiercely against attacks of other mammals, and the cubs quickly learn the value of speed – their main asset in both hunting and avoiding capture.

The running style of the cheetah

FACT FILE
PUMA (COUGAR, PANTHER)

Order:	Meateaters (Carnivora)
Family:	Felidae
Subfamily:	Felinae
Latin name:	*Felis concolor*
Colour:	Sandy or grey-brown, paler underneath; dark cheeks
Length:	Up to 2.4 m (8 ft)
Weight:	Up to 120 kg (260 lb)
Habitat:	Forest, woodland, plains, desert
Range:	Western Canada, USA, Central and South America

OCELOT

Order:	Meateaters (Carnivora)
Family:	Felidae
Subfamily:	Felinae
Latin name:	*Felis pardalis*
Colour:	Rich golden tawny, with black stripes and spots
Length:	1.3 m (4 ft 3 in)
Weight:	16 kg (35 lb)
Habitat:	Woodland, grassland
Range:	Southern USA, Mexico, Central America, eastern South America south to Uruguay

MARGAY

Order:	Meateaters (Carnivora)
Family:	Felidae
Subfamily:	Felinae
Latin name:	*Felis wiedi*
Colour:	Tawny, with black stripes and spots
Length:	1.1 m (3 ft 7 in)
Weight:	About 10 kg (22 lb)
Habitat:	Forests
Range:	Mexico, Central America, eastern South America south to Uruguay

MORE CATS OF THE AMERICAS

Pumas, ocelots and margays have been hunted and driven out by farmers, but still survive in wild areas.

PUMAS ARE NOT ONLY the largest cats of the subfamily Felinae, they are also among the most versatile and wide-ranging. They live in all kinds of habitat from dense forest to desert, throughout the Americas from the northern Rocky Mountains to southern Patagonia. They vary greatly in size, the largest living at the colder northern and southern ends of their range.

Pumas are plain-coloured rather than spotted or striped, varying in colour over their wide range from drab grey to rich tawny. Not surprisingly, they have been given many different names, including puma, cougar, catamount, painter and mountain lion. Their colours blend with most backgrounds, enabling them to creep up on unsuspecting prey. Their main food is deer, but they kill and eat a great variety of other mammals and birds. Big enough to take sheep and young cattle, they are never popular with farmers, who are usually allowed to kill them on sight.

Almost as big as lions, pumas look as though they should be able to roar. But they belong to the subfamily Felinae and, like house cats and others of the subfamily, they purr and squeal, but cannot roar. Like most other cats, they live alone in big, overlapping territories, coming together only briefly for mating. Pumas produce litters of three or four, sometimes up to six, kittens, and the mothers look after them for over a year.

Margay

Puma

Where they live

Puma and cubs

Ocelots are forest cats of the Americas, from the southern United States and Mexico to southern Brazil and Uruguay. Among the most beautiful of all cats, their skins are much in demand for furs. Shy animals, seldom venturing beyond the forest boundary, they hunt deer, peccaries and agoutis, usually running them down after a brief chase. From the trees they take monkeys, reptiles and birds.

Ocelots are unusual among cats in that males remain with females after mating. The two sometimes hunt together and keep in contact by calls within the territory. Litters are usually of one or two kittens, and the males contribute to family life by bringing food to the den.

Margays (also called long-tailed spotted cats) are similar to ocelots in colour and general appearance, though slightly smaller and lighter in build. They live in similar areas, but spend more time in the trees, taking a higher proportion of smaller mammals and birds. Like ocelots, they are shy, tending to keep well away from people. But their attractive skins are valued almost as highly as those of ocelots, and many thousands are killed each year.

Ocelot

Pumas originally roamed over much of North and South America. They retreated as forest clearing and farming spread across Canada and the United States. But today, even after several centuries of intensive hunting, they remain one of the most successful and widespread of all the large cats.

Neither ocelots nor margays have ever been so widespread in the north. Ocelots can still be found in the southern states of the United States but, like margays, they live mainly in forested country from Mexico south.

	Margay
	Ocelot
	Puma

RELATIONSHIPS

The subfamily Felinae is made up mainly of small cats, most of them close in size to house cats – some smaller and some a little larger. Just a few of the felines are big animals, approaching the size of leopards.

Ocelot with young

Pumas, ocelots and margays are three of the larger species, all of which live in different parts of North or South America.

Confusingly, pumas are also called panthers in parts of the Americas. This is an old name that was once given to big cats generally, and has stuck with American cats, even though they are now considered members of the Felinae rather than the Pantherinae.

WILD CATS OF THE AMERICAS

The forests and plains of North and South America are home to at least 11 species of cats, possibly more. These are all descended from ancestors that, long ago, made the crossing from Siberia to North America (see page 21), spreading first through North America and then south through Panama.

There are no lions, tigers or leopards among them. The only pantherine cats of the New World are North American lynxes and bobcats (shown on pages 22-23) and jaguars (24-25). Of the rest, some live in both North and South America, others only in South America. The three largest species are shown here, and six smaller species appear on the next two pages.

The narrow Isthmus of Panama has from time to time been broken by sea, isolating South America from the north. So although some of the southern cats live in North America, too, others live only in the south.

Margay, alert hunter of the forest

SMALLER CATS OF THE AMERICAS

Six different small cats populate the Americas, ranging from Texas in the north to the tip of Patagonia in the south.

FACT FILE

JAGUARUNDI

Order:	Meateaters (Carnivora)
Family:	Felidae
Subfamily:	Felinae
Latin name:	*Felis yagouaroundi*
Colour:	Plain, varying red-brown to grey
Length:	1 m (3 ft 3 in)
Weight:	7 kg (15 lb)
Habitat:	Grassland, scrub, swamps
Range:	Texas, Arizona, Mexico, Central America, South America to Uruguay

ANDEAN MOUNTAIN CAT

Order:	Meateaters (Carnivora)
Family:	Felidae
Subfamily:	Felinae
Latin name:	*Felis jacobita*
Colour:	Grey with dark spots and stripes
Length:	1 m (3 ft 3 in)
Weight:	4-7 kg (9-15 lb)
Habitat:	Dry alpine grasslands
Range:	Central Andes of Chile, Peru, Bolivia and northern Argentina

GEOFFROY'S CAT

Order:	Carnivora (meat-eaters)
Family:	Felidae
Subfamily:	Felinae
Latin name:	*Felis geoffroyi*
Colour:	Tawny yellow with black spots, striped face
Length:	95 cm (37 in)
Weight:	2-4 kg (4-9 lb)
Habitat:	Mountain forests
Range:	Bolivia, Paraguay, Argentina, southern Brazil, Uruguay

PAMPAS CAT

Order:	Meateaters (Carnivora)
Family:	Felidae
Subfamily:	Felinae
Latin name:	*Felis colocolo*
Colour:	Pale grey-brown with darker stripes
Length:	90 cm (35 in)
Weight:	3-7 kg (7-15 lb)
Habitat:	Temperate grasslands
Range:	Southern and west-central South America

KODKOD

Order:	Meateaters (Carnivora)
Family:	Felidae
Subfamily:	Felinae
Latin name:	*Felis guigna*
Colour:	Grey-brown, heavily spotted with black
Length:	67 cm (26 in)
Weight:	2.5 kg (5 lb 8 oz)
Habitat:	Mountain forests
Range:	Southern Chile and neighbouring Argentina

LITTLE SPOTTED CAT (ONCILLA)

Order:	Meateaters (Carnivora)
Family:	Felidae
Subfamily:	Felinae
Latin name:	*Felis tigrinus*
Colour:	Tawny with dark spots
Length:	85 cm (33 in)
Weight:	2.3 kg (5 lb 8 oz)
Habitat:	Woodlands
Range:	Central and northern South America

JAGUARUNDI ARE STRANGE-LOOKING CATS, long and slender in body and tail, but with short legs and broad head. Up to 1.2 m (4 ft) long, with plain brown or grey fur, they live in lowland forests, where they hunt birds, mice and other small animals. Those that live near water often fish along the banks or enter the water for a cooling swim. With their long sleek bodies and plain fur, they look more like otters than cats.

Unlike most other kinds of cats, jaguarundis often hunt in pairs. Where there is plenty of food, three or four may hunt over the same territory. Gestation lasts up to ten weeks, and three or four kittens make up each litter.

The Andean mountain cat is one of the least known of all the cats. It lives only in a small area of the high Andes mountains, and has never been properly studied by biologists. A grey cat with black bars and rings, it has long, fine fur that protects it from the extreme cold of the mountain winters. Andean mountain cats live in the alpine zone of thin, poor vegetation above the forests, at heights well over 3,000 m (10,000 ft). They feed on small mammals and birds. We know nothing of their reproduction or family life.

Andean mountain cat

Jaguarundi

Geoffroy's cat

Where they live

Geoffroy's cat, about the size of a house cat, lives in the southernmost forests and grasslands of South America. Named for a French naturalist, Geoffroy St Hilaire, who explored these areas in the early 1800s, it has a yellowish or grey coat, attractively spotted and striped with black. It has an unusually broad head. The backs of the ears are black, each with a prominent white spot. Geoffroy's cats are agile enough to climb trees, where they spend much of their time hunting birds and small mammals.

Pampas cats are pale grey or white, with yellow-grey blotches and dark brown or black spots and stripes. The fur is often long, with a distinctive mane around the neck. About the size of house cats, they live mainly on the pampas (grasslands) and in the forests. They feed on small mammals and birds, and produce litters of one or two kittens, rarely more. Living on open ground, they are easily hunted and trapped for their valuable furs.

Kodkods are tiny mountain cats, smaller than house cats, that live in the forests of southern Chile. Very little is known of their biology, or how they live. Grey-brown, with slightly tufted ears and striped tails, they hunt the forest floor for small rodents, but are equally adept at catching birds among the tree branches.

Pampas cat

Little spotted cats, too, are among the smallest of all cats, only half to three-quarters the size of a house cat. They live in open forest and woodland, taking readily to the trees where they hunt for birds, small rodents and lizards. They rear two or three kittens at a time, and are heavily hunted for their attractive spotted coats.

All the smaller cats of South America are difficult to see, either because they live in out-of-the-way places or because they are becoming rare from over-hunting. Many of them are kept in zoos, which may be the best places to see them.

Jaguarundis are found from the southern United States (Arizona and Texas) through Central America to southern Brazil, Paraguay and northern Argentina. Andean mountain cats are restricted to a very small area high in the mountains of Bolivia, Chile, Peru and northern Argentina, and kodkods to a similar small area of the high Andes further south.

Geoffroy's cats also occur high in the Andes of Bolivia and northern Argentina, but their range extends east across Brazil to Uruguay, and south to southern Patagonia.

Pampas cats have a more southerly range, from Ecuador to Chile, Argentina and Uruguay. Little spotted cats occur mainly in Colombia, Venezuela, Guyana, Brazil, Paraguay and northern Argentina.

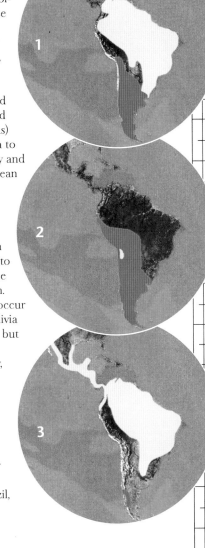

| 1. Little spotted cat 2. Andean mountain cat 3. Jaguarundi |
| 1. Geoffroy's cat 2. Pampas cat 3. Kodkod |

RELATIONSHIPS

Though all these cats are included in the genus *Felis*, some (for example, kodkods and Geoffroy's cats) are very similar to each other, while others (for example jaguarundis) are quite different in appearance from the others, and probably more distantly related.

Geoffroy's cat

Pampas cat

Kodkod

Little spotted cat

FACT FILE
EUROPEAN WILDCAT

Order:	Meateaters (Carnivora)
Family:	Felidae
Subfamily:	Felinae
Latin name:	*Felis silvestris*
Colour:	Dark yellow-grey, brown tabby stripes
Length:	85 cm (33 in)
Weight:	Up to 7 kg (15 lb)
Habitat:	Mountain woodland and forest
Range:	Western Europe east to Turkey and across Asia to China

AFRICAN WILDCAT

Order:	Meateaters (Carnivora)
Family:	Felidae
Subfamily:	Felinae
Latin name:	*Felis lybica*
Colour:	Very varied: black, grey, tan, ginger, tabby stripes
Length:	85 cm (33 in)
Weight:	Up to 7 kg (15 lb)
Habitat:	Grassland, forest, semidesert, mountains
Range:	North, east and south Africa, Middle East, Arabia, Mediterranean islands

WILDCATS OF THE OLD WORLD

The wildcats of Africa, Asia and Europe are fierce kin of the friendly house cat.

SEE AN ADULT EUROPEAN WILDCAT in the forest, and you might just mistake it for a house cat. At first it looks very similar – the same shape and size, and similar in colour and pattern to a domestic tabby. Look more closely and you will realize that the true wildcat has broader stripes, a bushier tail with rounded rather than pointed tip, and a larger skull, with bigger, staring eyes. The ears are more often flat than upright, a sign of fear when people are around. And, unless you have a special way of charming cats, no amount of calling will bring it to you.

European wildcats are so-called because they are best-known in Europe. The same species in several slightly different forms spreads far into western Asia as well. As many as 40 subspecies have been described. They may well have lived in these temperate forests and woodlands long before the coming of man. As the forests were invaded, cut down and burnt, and the land was cleared for farming, the wildcats retreated into the wilder places – the uplands and mountains where nobody wanted to live.

Though still widespread, there are fewer of them than before, and some of the remaining wildcats may be hybrids – crosses between wild and domestic cats. Wildcats feed mainly on birds and small mammals, including rats, mice, voles and squirrels. Though they mostly avoid places where there are people, occasionally one makes itself unpopular by attacking lambs, chickens, ducks and other farm stock.

BREEDING

Wildcats of both species live alone in small territories, which they mark with droppings and urine to let others know they are there. Females are ready to mate in early spring, in Europe usually between late February and April. Scent and calls attract several males, which follow for several days, calling noisily and fighting. Nine to ten weeks after mating, the mother finds a den or sheltered corner and gives birth to two or three kittens.

She feeds them on milk for about a month, gradually introducing them to meat, often to live prey that she has injured but not killed. So they learn to kill for themselves. Mother and kittens stay together for four to five months. Fathers take no part at all in bringing up the family.

African wildcat

Indian wildcat and kittens

African wildcats are similar in size but more varied in appearance. Their fur shows a range of colours from black to ginger-yellow, a variety that allows them to blend with a wide range of backgrounds, from forest to semidesert. Their colour patterns match those of house cats, as do their tails, which are slender and pointed rather than bushy. These are some of the reasons why biologists think that house cats are descended from African wildcats rather than European (see page 40).

Living in the drier areas of Africa and Arabia, they hunt very much like their European cousins, taking mainly small birds and mammals.

RELATIONSHIPS

If you see the kitten of a European or Asian wildcat on its own in the woods, you might easily mistake it for the lost or abandoned offspring of somebody's pet tabby cat. Pick it up, and you will discover your mistake. True wild cats are wild from the moment they are born. They may take food from you if they are hungry, and a warm corner if they are cold. But no amount of kindness and cosseting will turn wildcats into friendly, responsive house cats.

African wildcats, the second species listed here, are almost certainly the ancestors of house cats. Always more friendly towards man, they were tamed and trained to live close by in Egypt and the Middle East, and probably brought to Europe by the Romans. So your pet cat is the latest in a long line of cats that have been selected, generation after generation, for gentle behaviour and responsiveness to man.

Where they live

European wildcats that once roamed the continent freely are now restricted to remote forested areas of northern Scotland, Germany, France, Belgium, Spain, Portugal and eastern Europe. In Russia they are fairly plentiful in wild forests of the Caucasus Mountains.

African wildcats live throughout their continent, except in the driest deserts and the wettest equatorial forests. They extend also into Arabia, beyond into the Middle East, and as far as India. Wildcats of the Mediterranean islands also belong to this species.

 African wildcat

 European wildcat

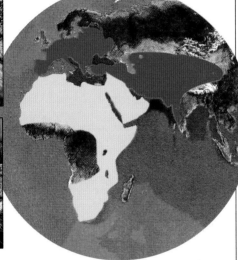

(Top) European wildcat
(Bottom) Scottish wildcat

European wildcat

FOES OR FRIENDS?

European farmers whose chickens disappeared overnight, and gamekeepers who lost young grouse and partridges that they were trying to rear, often blamed 'cats' for the losses. So they shot and trapped all cats, without much caring whether they were true wildcats or 'feral' cats - house or farm cats that had wandered or been driven from home and become wild.

This was not a good idea. One result was the gradual disappearance of true wildcats, and their replacement by feral cats, of which there was an unending supply. Another result was a plague of small mammals. For every chicken or game-bird that wildcats take, they also take many hundreds of mice, rats, rabbits and other small mammals that infest the fields and eat the crops. A better idea would have been to give the chickens and game birds better protection, and leave the cats to kill the vermin.

FACT FILE
SERVAL

Order:	Meateaters (Carnivora)
Family:	Felidae
Subfamily:	Felinae
Latin name:	*Felis serval*
Colour:	Pale fawn or cream with large black bars and spots
Length:	Up to 1 m (3 ft 3 in), including tail
Weight:	Up to 20 kg (44 lb)
Habitat:	Grassland, semidesert, forest
Range:	Northwest Africa and south of the Sahara

AFRICAN GOLDEN CAT

Order:	Meateaters (Carnivora)
Family:	Felidae
Subfamily:	Felinae
Latin name:	*Felis aurata*
Colour:	Sandy-brown with faint dark spots, head striped, paws dark
Length:	1.1 m (3 ft 7 in)
Weight:	14 kg (31 lb)
Habitat:	Deciduous tropical forest
Range:	Central Africa from Senegal to Kenya

SAND CAT

Order:	Meateaters (Carnivora)
Family:	Felidae
Subfamily:	Felinae
Latin name:	*Felis margarita*
Colour:	Golden-brown, paler underneath, striped head
Length:	75 cm (30 in)
Weight:	About 3 kg (7 lb)
Habitat:	Dry desert
Range:	North Africa, Arabia, southwestern Asia

BLACK-FOOTED CAT

Order:	Meateaters (Carnivora)
Family:	Felidae
Subfamily:	Felinae
Latin name:	*Felis negripes*
Colour:	Reddish brown, paler underneath, dark spots, black soles to feet
Length:	65 cm (26 in)
Weight:	About 2 kg (4 lb)
Habitat:	Grassland and semidesert
Range:	Kalahari Desert, Botswana, South Africa

SMALL CATS OF AFRICA

The serval, golden cat, sand cat and black-footed cat make their homes in four different African habitats.

SERVALS ARE TALL, thin cats, with long ears and long legs, and grey-to-brown fur spotted with black. They live in tall grass and desert scrub, resting during the heat of the day, and hunting mainly during the evening and early morning.

You may be lucky enough to see one hunting. It sits silently in the undergrowth, staring very intently at a point just ahead, listening carefully for the rustling of birds or small mammals among the grass. When the ears have pin-pointed the sound, it pounces, using claws and teeth to catch its prey. Servals can run and jump and climb trees, both to chase prey and to avoid being caught themselves by leopards and other predators.

African golden cats, by contrast, live in the dry deciduous forests south of the Sahara desert. Only a few have fur bright enough to be truly golden. Most are drab grey or dusty-brown, with slightly darker spots on the body. The head is striped, and the feet and backs of the ears are darker than the rest of the body.

Chunky animals, about twice the weight of house cats, they live mostly on the ground, but quickly climb trees to hunt or escape predators. They hunt mainly in the evening and early morning, taking rats, mice and other small rodents, and birds. Big ones are big enough to take small antelopes, too.

African golden cat

Serval

Sand cat

Sand cats can be any colour from reddish-brown to grey, with dark spots and stripes mainly on the face, flanks and tail. Their ears are wide-spaced,

Sand cat

the legs short, and the soles of the feet are covered with matted hair, making 'slippers' that protect them and give them a better grip on sand.

They live in desert and semidesert areas, mostly near oases or in dried-out water-courses where shrubs and grass provide cover, and food is more plentiful.

During the heat of the day, they live in burrows and under rocks to stay cool. At night they hunt insects, lizards, birds, mice and jerboas. Females produce four or more very small kittens, which grow quickly and in two or three months begin to forage for themselves.

Black-footed cats are similar to sand cats, but smaller and more darkly striped and spotted. The size of small house cats, they are probably the smallest of all wild cats, and perhaps the most solitary. They hunt alone, and seem to keep out of each other's way as much as possible. We know very little of their life in the wild. They live in grassland and semidesert, hunting at night for small birds, insects and mammals. Mothers produce two or three kittens to a litter.

Black-footed cat

Where they live

Servals live in semidesert scrub, grassland and marshes of southern Africa, south of the Sahara Desert. African golden cats also live south of the Sahara, but in a belt of deciduous forest that extends from the west coast to the Rift Valley of central east Africa. Sand cats are found in the Sahara itself, and in dry areas of Senegal and Egypt, and in Saudi Arabia. They, or other cats remarkably like them, are found, too, in desert areas east of the Caspian and Aral seas. Black-footed cats live in similar habitats further south, in the Kalahari Desert, Botswana and northern provinces of South Africa.

▨	1. African golden cat
	2. Black-footed cat
▨	1. Sand cat
	2. Serval

LIVING IN THE DESERT

Drinking water is one of the essentials of life, but a variety of reptiles, birds and mammals live in deserts where there is little or no water for them to drink. In these conditions, an animal's first precaution is to keep out of the sun as much as possible, so that its body does not become overheated. Cats sweat and pant to keep cool, just as we do, but both processes use up a lot of water. A safer way of living is to stay in the shade during the day, and hunt after sundown or in the early morning. In addition, during the chill of the night, enough dew may form on vegetation to give small animals a useful drink.

All plants and animals contain water. Indeed, about seven-tenths of the weight of a mammal is made up of water. So a cat that eats birds and mice is taking in valuable water as well. Many desert mammals have very efficient kidneys that produce especially concentrated urine, which again means that they are saving water.

RELATIONSHIPS

These four small African cats are probably quite closely related, but have evolved different ways of life. The two spotted species live mainly in grassland and among vegetation, where their spots and stripes help to hide them. The sand cats and golden cats closely match their sandy desert backgrounds.

African golden cat

LEOPARD CATS AND THEIR KIN

These five closely related species of small cats from southern Asia include one that fishes for its food.

FACT FILE

LEOPARD CAT

Order:	Meateaters (Carnivora)
Family:	Felidae
Subfamily:	Felinae
Latin name:	*Felis bengalensis*
Colour:	Varied: golden brown to fawn, with prominent black spots and stripes
Length:	90 cm (35 in)
Weight:	Up to 7 kg (15 lb)
Habitat:	Forests and woodlands
Range:	Northern India, Tibet, Nepal, China, Malaysia, Indonesia

IRIOMOTE CAT

Order:	Meateaters (Carnivora)
Family:	Felidae
Subfamily:	Felinae
Latin name:	*Felis iriomotensis*
Colour:	Dark brown, with black stripes and spots
Length:	80 cm (31 in)
Weight:	3.5 kg (8 lb)
Habitat:	Dense forest
Range:	Iriomote Island, south-west Japan

RUSTY-SPOTTED CAT

Order:	Meateaters (Carnivora)
Family:	Felidae
Subfamily:	Felinae
Latin name:	*Felis rubiginosus*
Colour:	Yellowish brown with brown spots
Length:	70 cm (28 in)
Weight:	1-2 kg (2-4 lb)
Habitat:	Forest, grassland, scrub
Range:	Southern India, Sri Lanka

FLAT-HEADED CAT

Order:	Meateaters (Carnivora)
Family:	Felidae
Subfamily:	Felinae
Latin name:	*Felis planiceps*
Colour:	Reddish brown, paler underneath, with white and black stripes on the face and head
Length:	70 cm (28 in)
Weight:	5-8 kg (11-18 lb)
Habitat:	Lowland plains, swamps and riverbanks
Range:	Sumatra, Borneo, Malaysia

FISHING CAT

Order:	Meateaters (Carnivora)
Family:	Felidae
Subfamily:	Felinae
Latin name:	*Felis viverrina*
Colour:	Reddish brown, with large black spots
Length:	1.1 m (3 ft 7 in)
Weight:	Up to 9 kg (20 lb)
Habitat:	Swamps and wetlands
Range:	India, Sri Lanka, Malaysia, Indonesia

Leopard cat with young

ABOUT THE SIZE OF HOUSE CATS, leopard cats are found over a wide area of southeastern Asia. Though varying much in colour and size, they have white, pale grey or yellowish fur, often heavily striped and spotted with black. The tail is short, the head small and round, often prettily marked with black and white stripes. The backs of the ears are black, with conspicuous white spots. Several local subspecies have been identified, especially on the islands within their range.

So-called for their spotted skin, leopard cats live in a wide variety of habitats, from dense forest to mountain scrub. They feed mainly on small rodents and birds. Big ones are strong enough to tackle small deer. Like most other cats, they live alone, coming together only for mating. Females give birth to two or three kittens, which live in a den, often in a hollow tree or small cave, for a month before emerging. Though protected in some parts of their range, many thousands are killed each year for their beautiful furs, in China especially.

Iriomote cat

Fishing cat

Rusty-spotted cat

Where they live

Iriomote cats live only on Iriomote, a small island in the Ryukyu group of southern Japan. In many ways they resemble leopard cats, but their legs are shorter and their fur is darker. They live in the lush forests that cover the island, and we know very little of how they live. As there cannot be more than about a hundred of them altogether, they are heavily protected.

Much smaller than either leopard or Iriomote cats, rusty-spotted cats have grey-brown fur, marked with faint stripes and spots of darker brown on the body, and stronger brown or black stripes on the head and face. In southern India, these cats live in grassland and scrub. In Sri Lanka, they are more likely to be found in forests. They lie up during the day and emerge at night to hunt rats, mice, bats and other small mammals, and birds.

Flat-headed cats, too, are small, with flattened and pointed head, long body, short, thick tail and short legs. The fur is reddish brown to silvery grey, much paler underneath, and the face is marked with prominent white stripes. They live near rivers and marshes, feeding nocturnally on fish, frogs and snails as well as small rodents and birds.

Fishing cats, largest of the group, are chunky animals with short legs and thick, short tails. Their fur is reddish brown, prominently marked with dark brown or black spots that merge into stripes on the shoulders, neck and face. They are usually found near water, and their name comes from their habit of scooping fish from streams with their front paws. Their toes are slightly webbed for this purpose.

Several observers have reported that fishing cats swim and dive in search of fish. However, they are known also to feed on reptiles, birds and rodents on dry land.

Leopard cat

Flat-headed cat

Leopard cats have a wide distribution, from western India, through northeastern India to southern China, from eastern China to Manchuria, and south to Malaysia, Borneo and the Philippine Islands. Iriomote cats occur only on Iriomote, a Japanese island east of Taiwan, and rusty-spotted cats are restricted to southern India and Sri Lanka.

Flat-headed cats are widespread in the Malay Peninsula, Sumatra and Borneo. Fishing cats occur in southern India and Sri Lanka, Burma, Bangladesh, Thailand, Java and Sumatra.

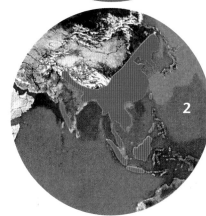

	1. Fishing cat 3. Flat-headed cat
	1. Iriomote cat 2. Leopard cat 3. Rusty-spotted cat

RELATIONSHIPS

These five closely related species of cats live in different parts of southern Asia. Some biologists think them so closely related that they separate them from the rest of the *Felis* cats and include them in a genus, *Prionailurus*, of their own. Wide-ranging leopard cats, about as big as house cats, are the basic stock. The cats of Iriomote Island, southern Japan, are a dark-furred local variation. Rusty-spotted and flat-headed cats are much smaller versions, while the fishing cats are relative giants.

CAN CATS SWIM?

House cats, the cats we are most familiar with, seem to hate water and keep away from it whenever they can. But there are several kinds of cats living near lakes, rivers and streams that certainly eat fish, and may enter the water to catch them. They probably find it better to stand in the shallows and scoop fish out with their paws, rather than chase after them. Only specially adapted mammals like otters and seals can outswim fish.

All mammals can swim if they fall into water. Most are better at it than we are, because they swim automatically and do not panic or use valuable energy in shouting for help. Cats are no exception. However, their fur is not waterproof, they can get very cold and wet, and not surprisingly they prefer to keep dry if they can. Putting your pet cat into water to see if it can swim is not a good idea. It can, but it will be a happier cat if you keep it warm and dry instead.

Malaysian fishing cat

FACT FILE

ASIAN GOLDEN CAT

Order:	Meateaters (Carnivora)
Family:	Felidae
Subfamily:	Felinae
Latin name:	*Felis temmincki*
Colour:	Varied: golden or reddish brown to grey, with dark stripes on the face
Length:	1.3 m (4 ft)
Weight:	6-11 kg (13-24 lb)
Habitat:	Forest, upland scrub
Range:	Nepal and Tibet, east to southern China, Malaysia, Sumatra

BAY CAT

Order:	Meateaters (Carnivora)
Family:	Felidae
Subfamily:	Felinae
Latin name:	*Felis badia*
Colour:	Reddish brown, with dark stripes on the face
Length:	1 m (3 ft 3 in)
Weight:	2-3 kg (4-7 lb)
Habitat:	Tropical forest edge
Range:	Borneo

JUNGLE CAT

Order:	Meateaters (Carnivora)
Family:	Felidae
Subfamily:	Felinae
Latin name:	*Felis chaus*
Colour:	Varied: reddish brown to sandy grey, dark stripes on forelegs, face and tail
Length:	1 m (3 ft 3 in)
Weight:	Up to 13.5 kg (30 lb)
Habitat:	Forest, swamps, wetlands
Range:	Middle East, Asia Minor, India, Sri Lanka, east to Malaysia

PALLAS'S CAT

Order:	Meateaters (Carnivora)
Family:	Felidae
Subfamily:	Felinae
Latin name:	*Felis manul*
Colour:	Grey or pale yellowish, with dark stripes on the face and tail
Length:	80 cm (31 in)
Weight:	3-5 kg (7-11 lb)
Habitat:	Desert, steppe, rocky plains
Range:	Asia Minor and Caspian Sea coast, east to Tibet and southern China

CHINESE DESERT CAT

Order:	Meateaters (Carnivora)
Family:	Felidae
Subfamily:	Felinae
Latin name:	*Felis bieti*
Colour:	Brown or yellow-grey, with faint spots and stripes
Length:	1 m (3 ft 3 in)
Weight:	About 5 kg (11 lb)
Habitat:	Semidesert, scrub
Range:	Eastern Tibet, southern China

Pallas's cat

MORE SMALL ASIAN CATS

Not much is known about these five species of cats from southern and southeastern Asia.

ASIAN GOLDEN CATS are slightly larger than their African cousins (pages 34-35), and like them can be any colour from golden brown to dull grey. Their heads have prominent dark spots and stripes. The bodies are more variable, faintly spotted or plain.

They live successfully both in forest and in open, rocky ground, hunting birds, mice, rats, hares and small deer. Their feeding ranges often extend onto farmland, and they can be a nuisance to farmers, taking chickens, goats, sheep and even buffalo calves. Mothers produce litters of two or three kittens.

Bay cats (also called Bornean red cats) are similar in shape to golden cats, and probably closely related. But they are much smaller, and seem to come in two colour forms, one with rich, reddish-brown fur, striped with black on the head and face, the other much paler. They live only on the island of Borneo, in rocky areas within dense forests, where there are very few people, and they are seldom seen. Not surprisingly, we know very little about them.

Asian golden cat

Pallas's cat

Jungle cat

Jungle cats are not well named. They live in tropical desert, scrub, grassland, reed-beds and forest – almost anywhere except the dense forests called jungle. Bigger and heavier than house cats, they vary greatly in colour, but are usually grey or brown, with just a few dark stripes on tail and legs, and with well-striped faces. The ears are slightly tufted like those of lynxes (pages 20-23), and many have long, shaggy fur, almost like Persian cats (page 41). They raise three or four kittens per litter, and feed on lizards, birds, hares, rodents and small deer.

Peter Simon Pallas, a German naturalist exploring near the Caspian Sea, discovered and named Pallas's cat over 220 years ago. Its alternative name is 'manul'. A long-haired grey-brown cat, with stripes mainly on the face and tail, it lives in semidesert scrub and grassland, hunting birds and small mammals. As many as five or six kittens are born in a litter.

Chinese desert cats, bigger and probably heavier than house cats, roam grassland, scrub and some semidesert areas of China. Grey-brown, with only slight spotting on the flanks, they have a few stripes on head and tail, and tufted lynx-like ears. Few studies have been made of them, so we know very little of how they live.

Asian golden cat

RELATIONSHIPS

Asian golden cats are very similar to African golden cats, and clearly very closely related. Some biologists regard them as belonging to the same species. Bay cats are similar again, perhaps just a smaller subspecies of golden cats, isolated on the island of Borneo. Jungle cats, Pallas's cats and Chinese desert cats seem to have evolved separately to take up slightly different ways of life over a wide range of habitats.

Chinese desert cat

Bay cat

Where they live

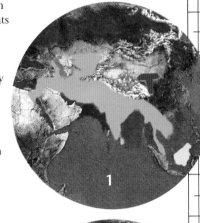

Asian golden cats live in a wide range of habitats from Nepal and Tibet to southeastern China, Thailand, Cambodia, Malaysia and Sumatra. Bay cats by contrast are found only in Borneo. Pallas's cats extend in a broad belt from east of the Caspian Sea and northern Iran to central China. Jungle cats live in an even wider range, from Egypt and the Middle East through southern Russia, India, Sri Lanka, Burma, Malaysia, Thailand and south-west China. Chinese desert cats are found only in western China, including Tibet, extending north into Mongolia.

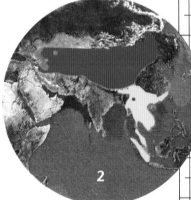

	1. Jungle cat
	1. Chinese desert cat 2. Pallas's cat
	1. Bay cat 2. Asian Golden cat

ISLAND SPECIES

Some species of cats are found over very wide regions of the earth, for example from the Middle East to China, while others are restricted to a single large island, like Borneo, or an even smaller island like Iriomote (pages 36-37). The wide-ranging species have existed for many millions of years, spreading through what was formerly a very uniform habitat. Changes in climate may have broken their habitat into dozens of separate areas, each with its own population, but the different populations have continued to interbreed. As a result, differences of size and colour between them have remained slight. Biologists judge them all still to be a single species, though perhaps in several subspecies.

When a species spreads to an island for the first time, it is usually just a few individuals that manage to get there, and they and their descendants can breed only among themselves. Conditions on the island may favour smaller or darker animals, or those with fewer spots or shorter tails. So the island cats gradually become different from those in the main stock, and biologists describing them for the first time judge them to be a separate species.

Jungle cat

FACT FILE

Order:	Meateaters (Carnivora)
Family:	Felidae
Subfamily:	Felinae
Latin name:	*Felis libyca domestica*
Colour:	Various
Length:	80 cm (31 in)
Weight:	3.5 kg (8 lb)
Habitat:	Houses, gardens, farms
Range:	Worldwide

RELATIONSHIPS

The common house cats we find all over the world are not a separate species. Biologists have traced their ancestry to the wildcats of northern Africa, which were first domesticated by the Egyptians some 3,500 years ago, and later taken all over Europe by travelling traders and soldiers. So they belong to the species *Felis libyca* (page 32), but are given their own subspecies, *domestica*.

Though some of them no longer look like wildcats, domesticated cats are still very similar to wildcats and other closely related small cats of Europe, Asia and Africa. Where house cats and wild cats live close to each other, they often interbreed. From such crossbreeding have arisen the many varieties of house cats that we know today, some of which are shown on this page.

Most of these varieties result from natural matings, but it is also possible for people who like particular kinds of domestic cats to 'improve the breed' by controlled breeding – making sure that only especially selected cats breed together. Siamese, Burmese and many of the long-haired varieties are bred in this way.

Red self-Persian, a pedigree breed

HOUSE CATS

Our pet cats originally came from Africa. Today they live all over the world, completely at home with their human friends.

THREE TO FOUR thousand years ago, farmers were growing seeds of wheat and other cereals for food, and storing the grain in their barns, some to be eaten and some to be saved for sowing the next year. Stored grain attracts rats and mice, which eat some of it and spoil the rest with their droppings. Where there is a good food supply, numbers of these rodent pests can build up within weeks from two or three to several hundreds.

Keeping a few cats around the houses and barns, feeding them from time to time and providing safe corners for their kittens, was a very good way of controlling rats and mice, and saving the harvest. The cats cost little to keep, and hardly had to change their ways – except to learn how to hunt their prey indoors, and not be frightened off when people were around.

Cats that hunted in barns and gardens produced kittens, which everybody loved for their playfulness.

Domestic cat with prey

Kittens that were handled and played with grew up into relaxed, happy cats that would sit by the fire and keep company with humans.

So cats became household pets as well as guardians of the barns. Even today, it is important to handle and play with kittens of house cats, to help them to accept humans and remain pets.

HOUSE CATS
(see picture and outline below)

1 **Tabby**	6 **Tortoiseshell**
2 **Tortie**	7 **Black**
& white	8 **Silver/grey**
3 **Marmalade/**	**tabby**
ginger	9 **Siamese**
4 **Persian**	10 **Black &**
5 **Burmese**	**white**

Domestic but wild

However tame and friendly, house cats are still partly wild. In their behaviour we can still recognize some of the habits and ways that helped their ancestors to survive in the wild.

Pet cats are still territorial. But instead of patrolling an area of mountain or woodland, their house and perhaps one or two gardens become their home territory. If other cats enter the territory, the 'owner' cat often becomes very tense and may even attack them. In the wild, both male cats (called toms) and females (queens) spray trees or rocks with their urine to warn other cats of their presence. House cats, especially toms, sometimes make themselves unpopular by spraying the table-legs or curtains instead.

Male house cats are often castrated (that is, the testes are removed by a vet) to make them quieter and less likely to fight. Similarly, females are spayed (ovaries removed) so that they cannot produce unwanted kittens. Females that have not been so treated, when they are ready to breed, attract males to the garden by scent and by calling noisily at

garage, spare room or cupboard – to produce her kittens. If you pay them too much attention, she may move them to another den, carrying them one at a time in her mouth. She may even hide them altogether, so you do not see them at all until she brings them out four or five weeks later.

Even well-fed cats may continue to hunt birds and small mammals. A pet female may sometimes bring a half-dead mouse or bird into the house and

Calico cat – patterned in gold, black and white

release it, giving a soft 'meow-wow-wow' call. In the wild, she would be bringing back prey to the den for her kittens, calling them around her to learn how to catch and kill for themselves.

Cat and owner snoozing in the mid-day heat

night. Four or five toms may respond, squealing and fighting among themselves. You often know when your own or your neighbour's cat is mating by the noise and disturbance at night.

Nine to ten weeks later the females produce two to four kittens. When about to give birth, your pet female may seek out a quiet, warm den – perhaps in the

House cats that are neglected or abandoned by their owners easily become feral (see page 33), or semi-wild. Unless they have grown fat and lazy, they are usually very capable of looking after themselves, living on rats, mice and small birds, scavenging food from dustbins, or visiting other houses where kind neighbours may leave food for them.

CATS AND PEOPLE

Wild cats have always hunted to live, but they have also been hunted by people for sport and are still killed for their furs.

TAMING THE HUNTERS

Caught as kittens and reared by hand, even lions and tigers can be tamed enough to become house pets – just so long as they remain small and cuddly. However, a lion only a few months old is already powerful, with strong claws and sharp teeth. Even a playful scratch or bite from a half-grown lion can inflict a serious wound, and a young lion that is cross, frightened or frustrated can kill.

The smaller of the big cats, such as cheetahs and jaguars, were once tamed and used to hunt other prey. In medieval times, kings and wealthy landowners in Africa, the Middle East, India and China kept stables of hunting cats, trained from kittenhood to live

among people, walk on leads, hunt when given the opportunity, and return willingly to their keepers. Big cats can also be trained to live in zoos and travel with circuses. There was a time when caged lions and tigers drew large crowds of onlookers, who had never before seen anything like them. People paid to see circus lion-tamers, with whips and uniforms, put these seemingly savage beasts through routines of tricks. Now that people can see videos and films of animals in the wild, there is less demand to see them in cages, or jumping on boxes in the circus ring.

MANY THOUSANDS OF YEARS AGO, when primitive people hunted in bands in the forests and plains, they must often have hunted alongside the big cats – lions, leopards, tigers, jaguars and cheetahs. They probably watched with envy as the cats chased and killed their prey. The animals were in every way more efficient than humans, with sharper eyesight and hearing, faster in the chase, and stronger at the kill. With their sharp teeth and claws, they were far better armed than men with their primitive spears.

Though rivals for the same food, people and the big cats sometimes learnt to co-operate. A band of men, like a band of hyenas or hunting dogs, could help to drive game towards a group of lions. Then, after the lions had killed and eaten to their satisfaction, the men could take their share of the meat. Until quite recently, this was the way that some African bushmen obtained some of their fresh meat.

Humans could also themselves become prey. To the big cats, they were just another kind of animal to be hunted. However, they were a kind that could strike back. We do not know when men first learnt to kill the big predators, but defending their homes and families would have been a strong reason for hunting and killing the individual animals that attacked human settlements.

RAIDING THE HERDS

Just a few thousand years ago, in Neolithic (New Stone Age) times, humans began to settle and farm the land, growing crops and herding cattle, sheep, goats and pigs. Some of the big cats, and the smaller ones, too, would have found domestic herds easier to hunt than wild ones. This forced herdsmen to post guards on their flocks during the day, and bring them into enclosures for safety at night.

At any time the herdsmen had to be ready to fight off raiding cats. Those men who killed lions, tigers or leopards with their spears would become local heroes. This battle continues today, wherever farmers graze their herds and flocks in country where big cats roam.

Often it is the older cats, perhaps crippled by disease or injury, and no longer able to hunt wild game, that turn to hunting the easier prey. Today they are not likely to last long. The herdsmen usually win.

HUNTING CATS FOR SPORT

Though men have always hunted and killed cats that were destroying their livestock, they have also hunted them purely for sport. This was a tradition among rulers of Africa and India, who set out with trains of

Mounted tiger head

huntsmen and followers – often to kill lions, tigers or leopards that had been hand-reared and released so that they could be shot.

Today, people travel just to see and photograph these animals, rather than shoot them.

Furs for fashion

In prehistoric times, before spinning and weaving were invented, humans living in cold climates often wore the furs of animals, usually those that they had killed for food. At first this was to keep warm. Later, some men came to feel that wearing skins of bears, leopards or lions made them as fearless as those animals.

Later still came the fashion for wearing rare or attractive furs for decoration. Today, very few people need to wear furs for warmth. We can usually keep warm in woven or knitted clothes. But in some places furs are still worn for decoration, and until recently many of the most popular furs were those of big or small cats.

When the fashion for fur

was at its height, wealthy women tended to choose the prettiest or most attractive ones, such as leopards, cheetahs, ocelots, marbled cats or little spotted wildcats. Over the years, this resulted in the destruction of many millions of cats, and the serious reduction or near-extinction of some of the most fashionable species or subspecies. Their deaths supported an industry that provided work for thousands of people, from skilled hunters to skin traders, designers, cutters, tailors, merchants and sales assistants.

Nowadays most people think it is wrong to kill wild animals for their furs. Others see no harm in it, and positive good in the amount of work it provides. What do you think?

Tiger skins in the fur trade

CATS IN MAGIC AND MEDICINE

In many parts of the world, cats were believed to have magic qualities. Witch's cats in Britain were thought to be friends of the devil, and different parts of cats were used to make magic or medicinal potions. Just as the skin of a tiger or leopard was thought to contain part of its spirit, so pieces of their bodies were – and still are – believed to make powerful medicines and cures.

Even today, throughout China and the Far East, dried and ground-up portions of tiger heart, liver, fat, bones, eyes, muscles, genital organs and whiskers can be bought on

market stalls. The buyers use them to make medicines that are supposed to cure all kinds of ills, from stiff joints to indigestion. Do they work? Millions of people believe they do, so hundreds of tigers die to keep up the supplies.

'Magic' tiger model

GLOSSARY

Can you identify the species pictured?
(answers below)

adapt	To change in ways that increase the chances of survival
aggressive	Likely to attack
ancestors	Parents, grandparents and earlier generations
barren land	Cold, dry areas, especially of the Arctic, where little vegetation grows
Bering Bridge	Dry land between northern Asia and North America, which existed when sea level was lower
carnivore	Animal that feeds mainly on the flesh of other animals
conservation	Saving and protecting species, usually by protecting the places where they live
deciduous forest	Forest in which most trees shed their leaves seasonally
density	Number (of animals or plants) in a particular area
digestive system	Parts of an animal in which food is broken down and absorbed (mouth, throat, stomach, intestines and so on)
dominant	Most important, able to control others
embryo	A baby growing inside its mother at a very early stage
feral	Feral cats are domesticated ones that have have run wild
forage	Search for food
fossil	Remnant of ancient plant or animal preserved in stone
fossil record	A series of fossils of different ages showing how a particular group of animals changed with time
genus	Group of closely related animals or plants (plural, genera)
gestation period	Length of time it takes for baby animals to grow inside their mother
habitat	Place where a plant or animal lives
herbivore	Animal that feeds mainly on vegetation (plant life)
mane	Long hair on the neck and shoulders
monitoring	Watching carefully to see what progress is being made
nocturnal	At night; describing animals that hunt or forage by night
panther	Alternative name for the leopard and also for the North American puma or cougar
pedigree	A pedigree animal or breed is one that has been bred from animals of the same kind and has a known ancestry

poachers	Illegal hunters
population	Part of a species living in a particular area, sometimes separated from other populations of the same species (see stock)
predator	Animal that hunts, kills and eats other animals
pregnant	Carrying a developing baby or babies inside the body
remnant	A population of animals left behind when most of the other members of the species have died out for some reason or another
retractile (claws)	Able to be withdrawn into protective sheaths
rodent	Mammal with sharp, chisel-like front teeth, such as a mouse, rat or squirrel
scavenge	Eat rubbish or old food that has been lying around for some time
scrub	A kind of vegetation composed mainly of bushes
species	A particular kind of plant or animal
stalk	Walk slowly and quietly after prey
stock	Small group of animals or plants of one species, forming part of a population (see population)
subspecies	A subdivision of a species, usually one living in a particular area and showing obvious differences from other populations of the same species; also called a race
testes	The male sex organs, which produce the sperm that fertilize the females' eggs
uterus	The womb, the part of a female's body in which the babies develop
vermin	Creatures, especially small ones such as mice and rats, that destroy or damage crops

Useful addresses	WWF (UK), Panda House, Weyside Park, Cattershall Lane, Godalming, Surrey GU7 1XR [Tel: (0)1483 426 444; Fax: (0)1483 426 409]
	WWF (USA), 1250 24th St NW, Suite 500, Washington DC 20037
	WWF (Australia), Level 5, 725 George Street, Sydney, NSW 2000
	WWF (South Africa), 116 Dorp Street, Stellenbosch 7600
	Wildlife Conservation International, New York Zoological Society 185th St and Southern Boulevard, Bronx, New York, NY 10460, USA
	Cat Specialist Group, World Conservation Union, Avenue de Mont-Blanc, CH-1196, Switzerland

From top: Clouded leopard, Scottish wildcat, lynx, tiger

INDEX